Criteria for Promotion and Tenure for Academic Librarians

CLIP Note #26

Compiled by

Virginia Vesper
Middle Tennessee State University
Murfreesboro, Tennessee

Gloria Kelley
Winthrop University
Rock Hill, South Carolina

College Library Information Packet Committee
College Libraries Section
Association of College and Research Libraries
A Division of the American Library Association
Chicago 1997

The paper used in this publication meets the minimum requirements of
American National Standard for Information Sciences–Permanence of
Paper for Printed Library Materials, ANSI Z39.48-1992. ∞

Library of Congress Cataloging-in-Publication Data
Vesper, Virginia.
 Criteria for promotion and tenure for academic librarians /
compiled by Virginia Vesper, Gloria Kelley.
  p. cm. -- (CLIP note ; #25)
 Includes bibliographical references (p.).
 ISBN 0-8389-7928-9 (alk. paper)
 1. College librarians--Promotions--United States. 2. College
librarians--Tenure--United States. I. Kelley, Gloria. II. Title.
III. Series.
Z682.4.C63V47   1997
023' .2--dc21   97-39396

Printed on recycled paper.

Printed in the United States of America.

01 00 99 98 97   5 4 3 2 1

Mon Mar 11 2002

Paging Slip

A request has been placed on the following item by the patron
listed below. Please pull this item and forward to the
location given below.

Heterick Memorial Library
Ohio Northern University
Ada, OH 45810

HML 3rd STACKS
CALL NO: 023.2 V579c
AUTHOR: Vesper, Virginia
Criteria for promotion and tenure f
BARCODE: 35111004346759
REC NO: i14501934
PICKUP AT: NEOUCOM

Rose Guerrieri
NEOUCOM-Information Center
INSTITUTION: NEOUCOM
LOCATION: ne2mh
PATRON TYPE: Faculty

TABLE OF CONTENTS

INTRODUCTION   1

SELECTED BIBLIOGRAPHY   9

CLIP NOTE SURVEY RESULTS   15

TENURE AND PROMOTION DOCUMENTS   31

    Public Institutions

        Arizona State University
        West Campus
        Phoenix, Arizona   35

        State University of New York College at Plattsburgh
        Plattsburgh, New York   64

    Private Institutions

        Alfred University
        Alfred, New York   75

        Eckerd College
        Saint Petersburg, Florida   86

        Saint Olaf College
        Northfield, Minnesota   93

    Document Involving Unions

        Trenton State College
        Trenton, New Jersey   99

Evaluation Forms

    Huntingdon College
    Montgomery, Alabama   109

    Wheaton College
    Wheaton, Illinois   112

    Tarleton State University
    Stephenville, Texas   115

Weighting of Criteria

    Widener University
    Chester, Pennsylvania   123

    State University of New York College at Geneseo
    Geneseo, New York   127

Supplement to Faculty Handbook

    Winthrop University
    Rock Hill, South Carolina   131

External Evaluation

    State University of New York College at New Paltz
    New Paltz, New York   141

CLIPNote Committee

The College Libraries Section CLIPNote Committee wishes to recognize the efforts of Lawrie Merz in bringing this volume to publication. Her vision, persistence, and editorial skills were invaluable in the development and completion of this project.

Elizabeth A. Sudduth, Chair
McGraw-Page Library
Randolph-Macon College
Ashland, Virginia

Roxann Bustos
Reese Library
Augusta State University
Augusta, Georgia

Jody L. Caldwell
Drew University Libraries
Drew University
Madison, New Jersey

Doralyn H. Edwards
Fondren Library
Rice University
Houston, Texas

Jamie Hastreiter
William Luther Cobb Library
Eckerd College
St. Petersburg, Florida

Lawrie Merz
Willard J. Houghton Library
Houghton College
Houghton, New York

Lewis R. Miller
Butler University Libraries
Butler University
Indianapolis, Indiana

INTRODUCTION

OBJECTIVE

The *College Library Information Packet (CLIP) Note* publishing program, under the auspices of the College Libraries Section of the Association of College and Research Libraries, provides "college and small university libraries with state-of-the-art reviews and current documentation on library practices and procedures of relevance to them" (Morein 1985). This *CLIP Note* provides information on criteria for tenure and promotion at academic institutions. The survey was sent to a predefined group of 265 small and medium sized academic libraries. The responding librarians are representative of the wide range in status and position among academic librarians, including librarians with faculty, staff, academic or administrative status.

BACKGROUND

The issues of tenure and promotion, while not exclusive to librarians with faculty status, have certainly been affected by the debate over the issue of faculty status for librarians. Although many acknowledge the library as the heart of the college or university, librarians are not so easily assigned a place and role in the academic community. The library literature is rife with articles discussing the role or status of the librarian on college and university campuses. The bibliography on pages 11-12 includes several articles on the pros and cons of faculty, academic, and professional status as well as other personnel issues regarding status. The status of librarians is an important question for many reasons. One of those reasons is that the the status of the librarian may be a determining factor in tenure and promotion eligibility, and this survey sought an answer to that question and others concerning tenure and promotion decisions for small and medium sized libraries.

Do librarians with faculty status have a greater opportunity for tenure and promotion than librarians with academic status or professional status? If librarians have faculty or academic status, which in itself is a major issue for discussion, should librarians be considered for tenure and promotion using criteria modeled after those applied to teaching faculty? Many librarians have recognized the need to have criteria for tenure and promotion in place that reflect the unique contributions of librarians on the university or college campus. Many libraries have developed criteria within their institution that assess librarians' distinctive responsibilities. Teaching, scholarship, and service have been interpreted differently for librarians by institutions in order to evaluate librarians' contributions appropriately. However, the library literature indicates that many librarians are not completely satisfied that their criteria adequately represent this role. Since librarians do not fit neatly into definitions of faculty, other professional standards and procedures for awarding promotion and job security have been used in some libraries. With the trend in higher education for evaluation and assessment, institutions and libraries need to examine their own criteria and procedures for granting tenure and offering the opportunity for promotion for librarians.

The purpose of this study was to gather information on current practices and to collect documents used for making decisions regarding tenure and promotion at academic institutions. The documents in this survey represent how the criteria are defined for librarians at other institutions, and will assist other libraries in creating or revising their own criteria for tenure and promotion that accurately reflect the unique role and responsibilities of the academic librarian.

SURVEY PROCEDURE

The procedure followed was the standard one for *CLIP Note* projects. The *CLIP Note* Committee of ACRL's College Libraries Section reviewed a proposal and drafts of a questionnaire. In September 1995, the survey was mailed to each of the 265 libraries that participate in the *CLIP Note* surveys. The tabulation of the results and the selection of documents were completed in the winter of 1995.

SURVEY RESULTS

A total of 185 responses to the questionnaire were received, a 70% response rate. Responses were received from 45 public and 140 private academic libraries. The average institutional size of survey respondents was 2,570 FTE students with 149.57 faculty, 7.32 librarians, and 11.26 support staff.

Status (Questions 5, 11)

The status of librarians at academic institutions is a complex issue, which is evident from the responses and comments to the questions on this survey. Questions 5-7, which addressed status, tenure and promotion confronted the issue directly. On the questionnaire, faculty status for librarians was defined as the acceptance of the same responsibilities and privileges as teaching faculty. Ninety-five, or 51% percent of the respondents indicated that they had faculty status. However, when asked in Question 6, if librarians are eligible for tenure, only 66 (36% of the 185 libraries responding to the survey) answered yes, indicating an ambiguity in the definition of faculty status among respondents. To further confuse the issue, librarians at only 68 responding libraries (37%) have academic rank, indicating that a number of the 95 libraries that have faculty status do not have corresponding academic rank. Another 53 (29%) have academic status, which includes *some* of the privileges of faculty. Librarians have administrative status at 72 institutions (39%) and staff status at 21 (11%). Five libraries specified that librarians have professional status with continuing appointments and rank. Four libraries indicated that they have both faculty and administrative staff as the result of a change in the status of librarians at their institutions from faculty to administrative staff.

It is clear from the variety of responses that librarians are grappling with the problem of status and rank at their institutions. The variations range from faculty status where librarians have all of the privileges and responsibilities with the exception of advising and student evaluations to that of staff status without promotion, rank, or continuing appointments. Responses to the survey indicate that without faculty status and/or academic rank, librarians are rarely eligible for tenure and promotion, thus the status of librarians is an important issue. In the responses to the survey, no libraries at which librarians have only administrative status indicated that librarians were eligible for tenure, and only 5 indicated the possibility of promotion. Of the 53 libraries with academic status for librarians, only two have tenure for librarians and 22 promotion. The question of faculty status becomes even more complex for the Director/Dean of the Library. Is this position faculty or administration? Almost every possible variation was reported in this survey. At one institution, the Director has administrative status, but the rest of the librarians have faculty status. In contrast, another institution reports that only the director has faculty status and is eligible for tenure. At yet another library, the director and unit heads have both administrative and faculty appointments and may be tenured. Some Library Directors/Deans responding to this survey included comments that reveal strong opinion and sentiment both for and against faculty status and academic rank.

Rankings (Question 11)

In all, 106 of the responding libraries (61%) had some sort of professorial or equivalent ranking for librarians. Sixty-eight, or 39% of the libraries responded that librarians are assigned professorial ranks. Thirty-eight, or 22% responded that they do not assign professorial ranks, but assign alternative titles or ranks including the Librarian I, II, III, 1V series, and titles that combined academic rank with the titles of Librarian, for example, Assistant Librarian or Associate Librarian. If one cannot judge a book by its cover, one should also not judge the status of a librarian by his/her title. At one private institution, librarians are professional staff but also considered to be members of the college faculty. Yet, the librarians do not have tenure and have the respective ranks of Librarian I, II, or III. On the flip side of that, librarians at one public institution have Librarian I, II, III rank with faculty status and tenure.

Tenure (Questions 6, 8-10, 31)

In Question 6, 66 of the 185 responding libraries or 36% indicated that their institutions grant tenure to all librarians. Answers to other questions about tenure in the survey may indicate a slightly different number depending in all cases upon the actual responses to the questions. These discrepancies are the result of several libraries that include library staff with faculty status and those with administrative status. The data indicate that at public institutions, librarians are more often considered eligible for tenure than at private institutions. Of the responding 45 public institutions, librarians at 31, or 69% are eligible for tenure; whereas at 140 private institutions, only 37, or 26% indicated that tenure was available to librarians. The data were also analyzed to determine if the size of the student enrollment correlates with tenure for librarians. The results indicate that tenure is more likely to be available at larger institutions with 32, or 48% of the 66 tenure-granting institutions with student enrollment above 3,000 FTE students. Where the student FTE was below 1,600, only 10 institutions grant tenure to librarians.

Question 9 addressed the issue of which librarians are eligible for tenure and promotion. Of the 137 respondents to the question, 69 libraries (50%; or 37% of the 185 libraries responding to the full survey) responded that all librarians are eligible for tenure and promotion. The number of responses is slightly more than the responses to a similar question in Question 6, a reflection of the ambiguity and confusion concerning terms such as faculty and academic status, the status of the Director/Dean, and the concept of tenure/continuing appointments. Another 30 (21%; or 16% of the 185 responding to the full survey) indicated all were eligible except for the Director, Dean and in one instance the Associate Dean. For the Deans, this reflects their administrative rather than faculty status. Two libraries grant tenure and promotion only to reference and public service librarians, a recognition of the emphasis on the teaching criteria necessary for tenure and promotion at many institutions. Question 31 asked what specific criteria are considered for tenure. There were 67 responses to this question, representing the number of institutions where librarians are eligible for tenure. The specific criteria for tenure most often checked on the survey in question 31 were job performance, by 64 libraries or 96% of the respondents to the question, publications by 64 (96%) and campus-wide committee assignments by 65 (97%). Also, considered as a high priority were participation in either national 61 (91%) or regional 59 (88%) organizations, and community service checked by 62 (93%).

Promotion (Questions 7, 27- 30)

Promotion is available for librarians at 113, or 61% of the 185 libraries returning surveys. Fifty-five, or 30%, indicated that librarians were not eligible for promotion. As with tenure, public institutions are more likely to promote librarians than private institutions. At 36 (80%) of the 45 public institutions, librarians are eligible for promotion, while at 77 (55%) of the 140 private institutions, librarians are eligible for promotion. The size of the institution determined by student FTE does not appear to significantly correlate with promotion for librarians, although librarians at larger institutions may have an advantage. The most interesting correlation is between promotion and status of librarians. Out of the 113 libraries in which librarians are promoted, 75%, or 85 libraries indicated that their librarians had faculty status, while, at 23 (20%), librarians have academic status or academic rank without faculty status. Only 5 institutions that promote librarians have administrative, staff, or professional status for librarians. Of the 95 libraries that indicated faculty status for at least one of the library staff (Question 6), 85 (89%) promote librarians, while of the 53 institutions in which librarians have academic status, 20 (38%) promote librarians.

Question 30 asked which criteria was considered for promotion, and libraries could check all answers that applied. Job performance is most often considered in promotion decisions by 99 of the responding libraries, or 89% of institutions in which librarians are promoted. A close second is participation in regional organizations, which is considered in promotion decisions by 97, or 86% of the libraries that promote librarians. Other criteria important for promotion decisions included campus-wide assignments considered by 95, or 84% of the institutions that promote librarians; presentations 95, or 84%; participating in national organizations 93, or 82%; and community service 92, or 81% of the institutions which promote librarians. Seven libraries indicated in comments that no specific criteria were considered for promotion. A comparison with question 31 (about criteria for tenure) points out the similarities in criteria except for publications, which are more important for tenure, according to the data.

Questions 27-29 evaluated the number of years of professional experience required for promotion. Ninety institutions, or 80% of the 113 institutions that promote librarians, specify the years of professional experience to be eligible for promotion to the next rank. Question 29 asked if the same number of years of professional experience are required for librarians as for teaching faculty: 77, or 68% of the 113 institutions that promote librarians, indicated that the years of professional experience required for librarians for promotion were the same as those of teaching faculty. When asked to specify the number of years required to be eligible for promotion to each rank, only 70 institutions responded, significantly lower than the 90 institutions above in Question 27 that indicated that they specify the number of years of experience for promotion. For the rank of assistant professor or the equivalent, three to five years was checked by 37 (53%) of the 70 respondents to that question; for associate professor or the equivalent, three to five years was checked by 36 (51%) of the 70 respondents to that question; and for professor or the equivalent, nine years or more was the response most often checked (46%) by respondents to that question.

Comparison of Criteria for Librarians and Teaching Faculty (Questions 14-15, 23-26)

The survey attempted to ascertain how the criteria for promotion and tenure for librarians were similar to or different from teaching faculty in questions 23-26. Only 49 libraries responded that teaching was a requirement for tenure and promotion, 43% of the 114[1] institutions that grant tenure and/or promotion to librarians. Of those 49 libraries, 23 (47%) responded that a separate definition was applied to teaching for librarians. Confusion about the teaching role and the definition of "teaching" is evident in the numerous comments gathered in this survey. Some definitions of teaching include supporting the educational mission of the university, teaching bibliographic instruction courses, teaching credit courses, but the majority of comments defined "teaching" as job performance, professional ability, or effectiveness as a librarian. Comments indicated that if libraries were not able to define this criterion as job performance, it created problems for librarians in the tenure process at their institution because few librarians were able to meet the criteria. Scholarship was indicated as

---

[1]Promotion is offered to librarians at 113 institutions; either tenure or promotion is offered to librarians at 114 institutions.

a requirement for tenure and promotion by 88 libraries, or 77% of the 114 institutions that grant tenure and/or offer promotion to librarians. Of those 88 libraries, only 14, or 16% indicated that a separate definition for scholarship was applied to librarians. Most of the comments defined scholarship as a continued commitment to professional growth and service. Service was indicated by 108, or 95% of the 114 institutions that grant tenure or offer promotion to librarians. Only 5 (4%) of those institutions have a separate definition for service for librarians. Service to the institution, the community, and the library profession are agreed upon by most institutions. Other criteria are considered for promotion and tenure at 60 institutions, or 53% of the 114 institutions that grant tenure and/or offer promotion to librarians, with the overwhelming majority listing job performance, professional growth, or skill in librarianship. Many of the private colleges with religious affiliation included a desire for a personal commitment to Christian values and/or beliefs from their faculty. Some institutions considered years of experience, service, and continuing educational growth.

Questions 14 and 15 considered whether libraries used the same criteria for tenure and promotion decisions for all librarians regardless of area of service, and whether these criteria for tenure and promotion were unique to the library or were campus-wide criteria. In 109, or 96% of the institutions that offer tenure and/or promotion to librarians, the library uses the same criteria regardless of area of service. In 47 institutions, or 41% of the 114 institutions that grant tenure and/or offer promotion, the library has separate criteria for tenure and promotion. Campus-wide criteria are used for the evaluation process at 85 institutions, or 75% of those institutions that offer tenure and/or promotion to librarians.

Terminal Degrees (Questions 12-13)

According to the ACRL, the M.L.S. is "the appropriate terminal professional degree for academic librarians." The responses indicated that the M.L.S. is considered as the terminal degree for 148, or 83% of academic librarians. When librarians are assigned ranks, 129 or (93%) of the responses indicated that, for the rank of Instructor or the equivalent, the M.L.S. is the required terminal degree. At the rank of Assistant Professor or the equivalent, 90% of the respondents require only the M.L.S. while 5 others, or 4%, also require a second master's degree. At the rank of Associate Professor or the equivalent, 103 (74%) of the institutions require the M.L.S., 21 (15%) a second master's and 6 (4%) a doctorate. For the rank of Professor, or the equivalent, 83 (60%) of institutions require the M.L.S., 20 (14%) a second master's, and 27 (19%) a doctorate. These statistics clearly show that the higher the professorial rank, the more the advanced degree or degrees will be required. Nonetheless, the majority of institutions accept the M.L.S. as the only degree necessary even at the highest rank.

Tenure and Promotion Decisions-makers (Questions 17-20)[2]

Tenure and promotion decisions involve both the library and institution. Libraries were asked to check a list of possible decision-makers in the tenure and promotion process. The four most important decision-making entities for the final promotion and tenure decision at the 114 institutions that offer tenure/promotion to librarians were: the Academic Vice-President (93, or 82%), the President (71, or 62%), the Dean/Library Director (74, or 65%), and the campus-wide committee (64, or 56%). Input into the tenure and promotion decision comes from a variety of sources at the 114 institutions that offer tenure/promotion to librarians: the Dean/Director of the library (104, or 91%), the Academic VP/Provost (90, or 79%), a campus-wide committee (65, or 57%), and the peer evaluation of other librarians and colleagues (38, or 33%), but input can include comments from teaching faculty, colleagues in the community or from another library, supervised staff, and students.

Libraries with their own tenure and promotion committees represent 31, or 27% of the 114 institutions that offer tenure/promotion to librarians. While public institutions comprise only a small percentage of the institutions surveyed, nevertheless, public institutions appear to be more likely than private institutions to have their own library tenure and promotion committee. The larger the institution, the more likely it will have its own committee since 26 of the 31 libraries that have their own tenure and promotion have student bodies of 3,000 or more. Representation on the campus-wide tenure and promotion committee or the possibility of election to the committee is indicated by 45 libraries, or 39% of those 114 institutions that grant tenure and/or promotion to librarians.

Of the 66 institutions in which librarians are eligible for tenure, 26 libraries (39%) have their own tenure and promotion committee, while, in 36 (55%), librarians are represented on campus-wide committees. Of the 113 institutions in which librarians are eligible for promotion, 28 (25%) have their own committee. The results of the survey indicate, then, that most tenure decisions (94%) for librarians involve a committee, whether internal or external to the library. While the majority of promotion decisions are also made by committee (64%), a considerable number are not, a fact that might warrant further study.

Conclusion

The survey found that 35% of the 185 responding institutions indicated that librarians were eligible for tenure and 61% were eligible for promotion. Librarians at public institutions were more often eligible for tenure than librarians at private institutions, and the data also indicates that the larger the institution, the more likely it is to grant tenure to librarians.

---

[2]For a more relevant interpretation of the data, percentages to questions 17-20 are based on the 114 institutions that offer tenure/promotion to librarians, rather than the actual number of respondents to the survey which included a significant number of responses from institutions where tenure/promotion was not offered.

However, the data clearly indicate that librarians with faculty status are more likely to be eligible for tenure than librarians with academic or administrative status. Only two institutions where librarians have academic status grant tenure to their librarians, and no institutions where librarians have administrative status grant tenure to librarians. The likelihood of promotion is also greater at a public institution and is more likely for librarians with faculty status. Eighty-nine percent of librarians with faculty status and 37% of librarians with academic status are eligible for promotion.

When librarians are evaluated for tenure and promotion, campus-wide criteria are used at 74% of those institutions which grant tenure/promotion to librarians, and 41% have developed their own criteria. Libraries, while using the campus-wide criteria for teaching faculty, are also willing to draft criteria that, while achieving parity with the teaching faculty, reflect the librarians' unique functions. A recurring complaint in library literature is that librarians are held to the same criteria as teaching faculty, yet are not given the release time to fulfill scholarship and publication criteria. The data from this survey indicate that the primary criteria used in evaluating librarians for tenure/promotion is job performance. For tenure, publications and participation in campus committees are also considered important criteria; for promotion, the emphasis is on professional participation in regional organizations and participation in campus committees. For the most part, librarians seem to be evaluated by criteria that are similar to teaching faculty, yet cognizant of the unique functions of the librarian.

It should be remembered that tenure and promotion criteria and decision-making are always done within the context of university governance. Librarians, as members of the academic community, regardless of their status, should have a voice in creating the criteria for tenure and promotion, as well as being a part of the decision-making.

SELECTED BIBLIOGRAPHY

SELECTED BIBLIOGRAPHY

Association of College and Research Libraries. Academic Status Committee. "Standards for Faculty Status for College and University Librarians." *College and Research Libraries News* 53 (May 1992): 317-18.

----------. "Statement on the Terminal Professional Degree for Academic Librarians. In *Academic Status: Statements and Resources, ed. Susan Kroll, 27.* Chicago: American Library Association, 1994.

Benedict, Marjorie A. "Librarians' Satisfaction with Faculty Status." *College and Research Libraries* 52 (November 1991): 538-48.

Black, William K., and Joan M. Leysen. "Scholarship and the Academic Librarian." *College and Research Libraries* 55 (May 1994): 229-41.

Budd, John. "Librarians are teachers." *Library Journal* 107 (October 15, 1982): 1944-46.

Buschman, John. "The Flip Side of Faculty Status." *College and Research Libraries News* 50 (December 1989): 972-76.

Creth, Sheila D. "Personnel Issues for Academic Librarians: A Review and Perspectives for the Future." *College and Research Libraries* 50 (March 1989): 144-52.

Cubberley, Carol W. *Tenure and Promotion for Academic Librarians: A Guidebook with Advice and Vignettes.* Jefferson, N.C.: McFarland & Co., 1996.

DeBoer, Kee, and Wendy Culotta. "The Academic Librarian and Faculty Status in the 1980s: A Survey of the Literature." *College and Research Libraries* 48 (May 1987): 215-23.

Dimmick, Judith A. "The Status of Faculty Status in Ohio Academic Libraries, 1990." Kent, Ohio: Kent State University, 1991. (ERIC Document Reproduction Service No. ED 339 392).

Gray, Becky Bolte, and Rosalee McReynolds. "A Comparison of Academic Librarians with and without Faculty Status in the Southeast." *College and Research Libraries* 44 (July 1983): 283-287.

Hill, Janet Swan. "Wearing Our Own Clothes: Librarians as Faculty." *The Journal of Academic Librarianship* 20 (May 1994): 71-76.

Kenny, Kathleen, Linda D. Tietjen, and Rutherford W. Witthus. "Increasing Scholarly Productivity among Library Faculty: Strategies for a Medium-Sized Library." *The Journal of Academic Librarianship* 16 (November 1990): 276-79.

Kingma, Bruce R., and Gilliam M. McCombs. "The Opportunity Costs of Faculty Status for Academic Librarians ." *College and Research Libraries* 56 (May 1995): 258-64.

Krompart, Janet. "Researching Faculty Status: A Selective Annotated Bibliography." *College and Research Libraries* 53 (September 1992): 439-49.

Lowry, Charles B. "The Status of Faculty Status for Academic Librarians: A Twenty-year Perspective." *College and Research Libraries* 54 (March 1993): 163-172.

McGowan, Julie J., and Elizabeth H. Dow. "Faculty Status and Academic Librarianship: Transformation to a Clinical Model." *Journal of Academic Librarianship* 21 (September 1995): 345-50.

Mitchell, W. Bede, and Bruce Morton. "On Becoming Faculty Librarians: Acculturation Problems and Remedies." *College and Research Libraries* 53 (September 1992): 379-92.

Morein, P. Grady. "What is a CLIP Note?" *College and Research Libraries News* 46 (1985): 226-229.

Park, Elizabeth, and Robert Riggs. "Tenure and Promotion: A Study of Practices by Institutional Type," *Journal of Academic Librarianship* 19 (May 1993): 72-77.

-----------. "Status of the Profession: A 1989 National Survey of Tenure and Promotion Policies for Academic Librarians." *College and Research Libraries* 52 (May 1991): 275-89.

Payne, Joyce, and Janet Wagner. "Librarians, Publication, and Tenure." *College and Research Libraries* 45 (May 1984): 133-39.

Savage, Daniel A. "Bibliography on Academic and/or Faculty Status for Librarians." Ancaster, Ontario: Redeemer College, January 1992. (ERIC Document Reproduction Service, No. ED 344 590).

Shapiro, Beth J. "The Myths Surrounding Faculty Status for Librarians." *College and Research Libraries News* 54 (November 1993): 562-3.

Siggins, Jack A. "Academic Status for Librarians in ARL Libraries." *SPEC KIT #182.* Washington, D.C.: Association of Research Libraries. Office of Management Services. March 1992.

Turner, Bonnie L., and Ellen I. Watson. "Promotion and Tenure for Library Faculty." Peoria, IL: Bradley University, 1989. (ERIC Document Reproduction Service No. ED 331 504).

Watson, Ellen I. "Guidelines for Promotion and Tenure for Library Faculty." Peoria, IL:
    Bardley University, 1993. (ERIC Document Reproduction Service No. ED 372 769).

Werrell, Emily, and Laura A. Sullivan. "Faculty Status for Academic Librarians: A Review
    of the Literature." *College and Research Libraries* 48 (March 1987): 95-103.

CLIP Note **SURVEY RESULTS**

CLIP Notes SURVEY RESULTS

INSTITUTIONAL AND LIBRARY PROFILE: FY 1994/95

Institutions: Public 45   Private 140

1. Number of full time equivalent students
    185 respondents
    2570 (mean)
    2000 (median)
    Range 8869 The highest number of full-time equivalent students is 9,391; the lowest number is 522.

2. Number of full time equivalent faculty
    185 respondents
    149.57 (mean)
    134 (median)
    Range 384.5 with the highest number of full time equivalent faculty 415; the lowest number is 30.5.

3. Number of full time equivalent librarians
    185 respondents
    7.32 (mean)
    6 (median)
    Range 19.6 with the highest number of full time equivalent librarians 20.6; the lowest number is 1.

4. Number of full time equivalent support staff in library
    185 respondents
    11.26 (mean)
    9 (median)
    Range 46.5 with the highest number of full time equivalent support staff in the library   47.5 and the lowest number is 1.

5. Check the following as it applies to your librarians:
   185 respondents
   a. faculty status   95 (51%)
   (Faculty status implies the acceptance of the same responsibilities and privileges as teaching faculty)
   b. academic rank   68 (37%)
   (Holds title of instructor, assistant, associate or full professor)
   c. academic status   53 (29%)
   (Librarians share some faculty privileges)
   d. administrative status   72 (39%)
   e. staff status   21 (11%)
   f. other:
       professional staff status   4 (2%)
       exempt staff status   1 (5%)
       Academic professionals, eligible for continuing appointments and rank in a library series   1 (5%)

6. If the librarians at your institution are considered faculty, are they eligible for tenure?
   147 respondents
   Yes   66 (45%)
   No   74 (50%)
   Other   7 (5%)
       Continuing appointments instead of tenure   4 (3%)
       No tenure for any faculty   3 (2%)
       Tenure for library faculty except for director   2 (1%)
       Only the director eligible for tenure   2 (1%)

7. Are the librarians at your institution eligible for promotion?
   172 respondents
   Yes   113 (66%)
   No   55 (32%)
   Other   4 (2%)
       Yes, only director
       No, not in rank
       Not at this time
       Negotiating

8. Is there a separate track for librarians for promotion and tenure at your institution?
   157 respondents
   Yes   32 (20%)
   No   122 (78%)
   Other   3 (2%)
       Under revision
       Policy in draft
       Not clear

9. Which professional librarians at your institution are eligible for tenure and promotion?
   137 respondents

Library Director	7 (5%)
All	69 (50%)
Other	7 (5%)
All except the Director	27 (20%)
None	16 (12%)
All, only for promotion	9 (7%)
Director and Reference Librarians only	1 (.7%)
All library faculty are reference/public service librarians	1 (.7%)
Public Services Librarians	1 (.7%)
Technical Services Librarians	1 (.7%)
Unit Heads	1 (.7%)
Reference Librarians	1 (.7%)
Systems Librarians	1 (.7%)
All except the Director for promotion	1 (.7%)
Only those in faculty track	1 (.7%)
Librarian have tenure only at full professor rank	1 (.7%)
Positions are eligible for regarding as part of the position classification system	1 (.7%)

10. Is one general set of criteria used for promotion and/or tenure for all librarians regardless of area of service?
    136 respondents

Yes	109 (80%)
No	26 (19%)
Other	1 (.7%)

11. Are the librarians at your institution assigned professorial rankings?
    173 respondents

Yes	68 (39%)
No	67 (39%)
Other	38 (22%)

If not, what titles/rankings are applied to librarians?

Librarians I, II, III, IV or IV, III, II, I	11 (6%)
Affiliate Librarian or Instructor, Assistant Librarian, (Senior Assistant Librarian)	
Associate Librarian, Librarian or Senior Librarian	21 (12%)

12. Is the M.L.S. degree considered the terminal degree for librarians at your institution?

178 respondents

Yes	148	(83%)
No	20	(11%)
Other	10	(6%)

13. What is the highest degree required for librarians at each rank? Check highest required degree for each rank. If your librarians are not assigned professorial ranks, please substitute the appropriate equivalent on lines provided below each rank.

139 respondents

Instructor (Librarian I)

M.L.S.	129	(93%)

Assistant Professor (Assistant Librarian, Librarian II)

M.L.S.	125	(90%)
Second Master's	5	(4%)

Associate Professor (Associate Librarian, Librarian III)

M.L.S.	103	(74%)
Second Master's	21	(15%)
Doctorate	6	(4%)

Professor (Librarian, Senior Librarian, Librarian IV)

M.L.S.	83	(60%)
Second Master's	20	(14%)
Doctorate	27	(19%)

14. Is there a campus-wide statement of criteria for promotion and tenure used throughout   your institution (i.e. including librarians)?
(Librarian, Senior Librarian, Librarian IV)

151 respondents

Yes	85	(56%)
No	63	(42%)
Other	3	(2%)

If so, was a librarian included in the development of the campus-wide statement?

102 respondents

Yes	51	(50%)
No	47	(46%)
Other	4	(4%)

15. Does the library have a separate statement of criteria for granting promotion and tenure for its librarians?

150 respondents

Yes	47 (31%)
No	102 (68%)
Other	1 (.7%)

Comments:

Librarians are evaluated by "in house" and "campus-wide" criteria.

Use modified version of campus statement.

Some of the rank and promotion criteria does not apply to librarian, the Vice-President for Academic Affairs says that librarians will be considered on a case by case basis using previous standards, years and supervisor's recommendations.

16. If the library has a separate statement, who wrote the policy governing promotion and   tenure for librarians? Check all that apply.

56 respondents

Library committee	26 (46%)
Library Dean/Director	14 (25%)
Other	20 (36%)

All librarians

Union and administration representative

Whole staff

Library faculty

Library Director with input from the College Dean and President

Librarians, Director, faculty representatives committee

Faculty Handbook Committee

Faculty Committee

Promotion and Tenure Committee

Reviewed by administration and Board of Trustees

Ad Hoc Committee

Librarians and Dean of College

Academic Vice-President

Library Committee and library staff

17. Does the library have its own tenure and promotion committee?

155 respondents

Yes	31 (20%)
No	123 (79%)
Other	1 (.6%)

18. Does the library have representation on the campus-wide tenure and promotion committee?

165 respondents

Yes	45	(27%)
No	100	(61%)
Other	20	(12%)

19. Who makes the promotion and tenure decisions for librarians? Check all that apply.

127 respondents

Academic Vice President	93	(73%)
Library Dean/Director	74	(58%)
President	71	(56%)
Campus-wide committee	64	(50%)
Library promotion/tenure Committee	38	(30%)
Board of Trustees	17	(13%)
Personnel Office	2	(2%)
Union	0	(0%)
Other	24	(19%)

    Dean of student, Vice-President for Development, VP for Administration
    All librarians
    Faculty Committee
    Special tenure committee for librarians
    Faculty Personnel Committee
    No rank or promotion
    Campus-wide Committee is the final authority
    Under review
    College where librarian has faculty appointment
    Board of Directors
    Immediate supervisor
    Council of Deans
    State Board of Agriculture
    Peer Committee
    Promotion committee of the Board of Trustees
    Library Committee
    Library Faculty
    Chancellor

20. Who has input into the promotion and tenure decisions? Check all that apply.
127 respondents

Library Director/Dean	104 (82%)
Academic Vice President/Provost	90 (71%)
Campus-wide committee	65 (51%)
President	51 (40%)
Library promotion/tenure committee	38 (30%)
Trustees	4 (3%)
Personnel Officer	3 (2%)
Unions	1 (.8%)
Other	27 (21%)

Dean of Students, Vice-President for Development, Vice-President for Administration
Faculty Committee
Other librarians, faculty, students
All librarians
Special tenure committee for librarians
Department heads
Librarians and faculty
Other faculty
Outside references
Colleagues
Departmental staff
Department chairs
Committee of Deans
Peer committee
Faculty and peers
Colleagues and faculty

21. Are librarians at your institution eligible for grants and/or sabbaticals of the same length as teaching faculty?
155 respondents

Faculty Development Grants	112 (72%)
Institutional professional development grants	97 (63%)
Sabbaticals	92 (59%)
Other	30 (19%)
None	6 (4%)

22. Are librarians at your institution eligible for sabbaticals of the same length as teaching   faculty?
155 respondents
Yes   79 (51%)
No   67 (43%)
Other   9 (6%)

If they are different, are they shorter or longer?
17 respondents
Longer   2 (12%)
Shorter   15 (88%)

23. Is teaching part of the requirement for promotion or tenure?
127 respondents
Yes   49 (39%)
No   78 (61%)

If so, is a separate definition of teaching applied to librarians?
52 respondents
Yes   23 (44%)
No   29 (56%)

Comments:
   Teaching applies to formal bibliographic instruction.
   Teaching is the equivalent of a librarian's professional work.
   Effectiveness in performance, professional ability.
   Evidence of continuing effective support of the teaching-learning process
   We recognize the teaching role of librarians in bibliographic instruction and
      reference service.
   Professional service is substituted for teaching
   The three main criteria for promotion are the same for faculty and librarians
      with one exception: for faculty teaching is the first consideration, for
      librarian, job performance and effectiveness.
   Effectiveness in performance, professional ability.
   All faculty librarians have a heavy teaching load. Every incoming student is
      required to take a six-week seminar--librarians do two hours of
      instruction in every section plus all English 102 plus first course in
      major and senior seminar, all graduate research.
   No specific definition has been developed, but all professional librarians here
      are considered to be teachers on a one-to-one basis.

24. Is scholarship part of the requirement for promotion or tenure?
121 respondents

Yes	88	(73%)
No	33	(27%)

If so, is a separate definition of scholarship applied to librarians?
79 respondents

Yes	14	(18%)
No	65	(82%)

Comments:

Professional and scholarly contribution to Library Science or of the respective disciplines of the librarians.

Scholarship at the librarian rank involves more in-depth problem analysis, and or publication of bibliographies, literature reviews and creative articles externally rather in-house. Publications and presentation may be either in the discipline of the librarianship or a discipline corresponding to subject assignment.

A demonstrated concern for advancing and improving the level of the professional expertise and services through additional graduate study, work as a consultant, presentations, contributions to publication, leadership in local, regional, an national professional organizations, or attendance at conferences.

At the Associate Librarian rank, publication is more likely to take the form of presentation of descriptive papers at professional meeting, in-house problem analyses, preparation of more formal guides to the literature for specific classes, or publication of book reviews and information columns in section newsletters of professional associations.

Activities that impact and advance both the practice and science of librarianship.

Scholarship is not as stringent as for teaching faculty because librarians are on a 12 month contract; no release time for research or funds for providing scholarship strategies.

Contributions to the profession, including publications, papers presented, participation in professional organizations.

Articles in library journals do not count.

Professional activity and development.

Scholarship is broadly defined.

Includes professional service

Not necessarily publications

25. Is service part of the requirement for promotion or tenure?
   123 respondents
   Yes   108 (88%)
   No   15 (12%)

   If so, is a separate definition of service applied to librarians?
   87 respondents
   Yes   5 (6%)
   No   82 (94%)

   Comments:
   Must document significant professional contributions and value to the operation of
       the Library and University.
   Includes involvement in professional organizations, campus, library, and
       university wide committees, other community service such as library
       boards, literacy volunteers, etc.
   A demonstrated record of participation in library and college governance,
       participation in professional organizations, community outreach efforts,
       and civic service groups.
   Service to institution, community, and to the library profession
   Faculty librarians can be candidates for all faculty committees and have
       served on the University Curriculum Committee as well as Faculty
       Senate.

26. Are criteria other than teaching, scholarship, and service considered for promotion and tenure?

119 respondents

Yes	60	(50%)
No	59	(50%)
Job performance & professional activities	14	(12%)
Professional growth and development	4	(3%)
Equate job with teaching	2	(2%)

Other

Performance, seniority

Skill in librarianship and, if applicable, supervisory and leadership skills

Christian witness, degree of responsibility in the work of the college,
   professional reputation, devoting to teaching and inquiry.

Portfolio contributions and professional development.

Job performance, student development.

Advising and professional development.

Administrative responsibility.

Professional effectiveness.

Personal integrity and search for values.

Education level.

Contribute to mission of the college -- good character or citizenship.

Excellence in library work.

Credit classes, general attitude and Christian commitment.

Foreign travel.

Length of service at each rank.

Mastery of subject matter - continuing growth.

27. Do the criteria for promotion at your institution specify the years of professional experience to be eligible for promotion to the next rank?

122 respondents

Yes	90	(74%)
No	32	(26%)

28. If so how many years of professional experience (either at another institution or in rank at your institution) are required to be eligible for promotion to each rank? Indicate number of years in the space provided.
70 respondents
Assistant Professor (or equivalent)
0-2 years	27	(39%)
3-5 years	37	(53%)
6 +years	6	(9%)

Associate Professor (or equivalent)
3-5 years	36	(51%)
6-8 years	31	(44%)
9 + years	3	(4%)

Professor (or equivalent)
3-5 years	19	(27%)
6-8 years	19	(27%)
9 + years	32	(46%)

29. Are the years of professional experience required of librarians for promotion the same as those for teaching faculty?
110 respondents
Yes	77	(70%)
No	33	(30%)

If they are different, are fewer or more years in rank required of librarians?
20 respondents
More	11	(55%)
Fewer	7	(35%)
Other	2	(10%)

30. Which criteria do you consider for promotion? Check all that apply.

125 respondents

Job performance	99 (79%)
Participating in Regional Organizations	97 (78%)
Campus-wide Committee Assignments	95 (76%)
Presentations	95 (76%)
Participating in National Organizations	93 (74%)
Community service	92 (74%)
Workshops	90 (72%)
Publications	87 (70%)
Teach library instruction	85 (68%)
Library Committee Assignments	83 (66%)
Consulting	67 (54%)
Technology classes/courses	55 (44%)
Teach credit courses	51 (41%)
Statement	30 (24%)

31. Which criteria does your institution consider for tenure? Check all that apply.

67 respondents

Campus-wide Committee Assignments	65 (97%)
Job performance	64 (96%)
Publications	64 (96%)
Community service	62 (93%)
Participating in National Organizations	61 (91%)
Participating in Regional Organizations	59 (88%)
Presentations	59 (88%)
Library Committee Assignments	57 (85%)
Workshops	57 (85%)
Teach library instruction	53 (79%)
Consulting	45 (67%)
Teach credit courses	41 (61%)
Technology classes/courses	38 (57%)
Statement	24 (36%)

TENURE AND PROMOTION DOCUMENTS

Public Institutions

Arizona State University
West Campus
Phoenix, Arizona

State University of New York College at Plattsburgh
Plattsburgh, New York

Arizona State University West
Library

Policies and Procedures Governing

the Award of and Progress toward

Continuing Appointment

and

Promotion in Rank

Amended and Adopted by Librarians' Caucus
July 21, 1993

Amended
August 24, 1993

Amended
August 8, 1995

Approved by Dean of the Library   _____

Approved by Vice Provost for Academic
    Personnel   _____

Approved by Provost   _____

Introduction

Policies and procedures relating to evaluation of (a) meritorious performance, (b) progress toward and award of continuing appointment, and (c) promotion in rank shall be based on the following general principles.

1. The process and standards of evaluation shall serve the purpose of (a) providing quality library programs and services, (b) fostering individual growth and development, and (c) encouraging program development and innovation.

2. There should be consistency between judgments on merit and the award of continuing appointment and promotion except as outlined in ACDW.

3. Within the stated criteria, there shall be viable and alternative tracks to the award of continuing appointment and promotion in rank.

4. Supervisors and peers are responsible for: (a) making professional judgments, (b) counseling individuals on their performance and career strategies, and (c) advising individuals as to institutional expectations. Such guidance, however, cannot serve as a guarantee of award of merit, continuing appointment nor promotion.

5. Colleagues are important judges of performance in the areas of position effectiveness, professional contributions, and service. Therefore their recommendations will be central to decisions on appointment, retention, promotion, and the award of continuing appointment.

6. The individual is responsible for presenting evidence of having met the evaluation standards.

7. Individual career-development strategies should include activities for which there can be evidence of recognition by the profession at large.

Peer Review Policies and Procedures

I. Review Committees

A. Peer Review Committee

1. Duties

a. In accordance with the policies and procedures as outlined by ABOR, ACD, ACDW, and the ASU West Library, the committee will:

(1) make recommendations for continuing appointment and promotion;

(2) recommend rank and status (probationary or continuing appointment) at time of appointment;

(3) review Second and Fourth year probationary librarians and make recommendations on questions of reappointment; and

(4) make recommendations as to Emeritus status of retiring librarians.

All recommendations will be submitted in writing to the Dean of the Library.

b. The Committee will also:

(1) Monitor procedures and calendar for each year;

(2) Confer with the Dean of the Library concerning policy and procedure, and as specified by the review procedures document;

(3) Present an annual report to the ASU West Librarians Caucus during the spring semester of each year.

2. Membership

a. The Committee will consist of five West librarians with continuing appointment, one of which must hold Librarian rank.

b. Until there is sufficient pool of West librarians to ensure this committee makeup, the Committee will consist of

(1) all West librarians with continuing appointment, holding senior rank.

(2) a full librarian from ASU Main.

(3) a second full librarian from ASU Main to be added when a candidate is applying to full librarian.

(4) a minimum of three voting members

    c.   Committee members are ineligible to review and make recommendations on

        (1)   themselves,

        (2)   cases in which participation would create a condition of double jeopardy, (Supervisors or ASU West P & T Committee)

        (3)   cases in which participation would create a condition of potential conflict of interest for that individual.

    d.   Candidates have the right to challenge participation by an individual when they feel that participation represents a potential bias in the consideration of their case.

    e.   Challenges will be filed in writing to the Dean whose decision will be final.

    f.   Committee members will be elected annually by the ASU West Librarians Caucus. The method of election shall be by written ballot.

    g.   The Chair of the ASU West Librarians Caucus will report the results of the Peer Review Committee election to the Dean of the Library by a date designated by the Dean.

3.   Officers

    a.   The chair will be elected at the first meeting of the Committee and shall be an ASU West member holding continuing appointment.

    b.   The chair or his/her designee will act as secretary during deliberations.

    c.   The chair will be charged with establishing the agenda for meetings, presiding over meetings, acting as spokesperson for the Committee, and preparing the necessary reports and recommendations.

4.   Meetings

    a.   Meetings of the Committee will be called by the Chair as deemed necessary to conduct business.

    b.   The first meeting of the year will be called by the previous year's Committee chair or the Chair of the ASU West Librarians Caucus if the Committee Chair is unavailable.

    c.   Meetings will be closed and proceedings confidential.

    d.   A quorum of more than 50% will be necessary to conduct Committee business. Until the ASU West Librarians have a sufficient pool of librarians to ensure a committee constituted as described above, a quorum will be defined as 100% of the members.

B. **ASU West Promotion and Tenure Committee**

   1.   Membership

      a.   Librarians holding senior rank and continuing appointment will be eligible for nomination to this committee.

   2.   Election

      a.   A slate of nominees will be elected by the ASU West Librarians Caucus.

      b.   The Chair of the ASU West Librarians Caucus will notify the Dean of the Library of the nominees prior to the date the names need to be forwarded to the Provost.

II.   Review Procedures

A.   **General Policy**

These procedures will be consistent with the "ASU West Handbook for Faculty and Academic Professionals" and the Schedule of Personnel Action distributed by the Office of the Vice Provost for Academic Personnel.

B.   **Schedule**

   1.   The Dean of the Library will distribute to all librarians these annually updated documents which outline dates by which steps shall be completed:

      a.   ASU West Academic Affairs *Schedule of Personnel Actions, Faculty and Academic Professionals*

      b.   ASU West Library *Schedule of Personnel Actions.*

      c.   ASU West Library *Calendar of Scheduled Reviews*

   2.   On or before the date review files are due to the Peer Review Committee, the Dean of the Library will provide to the Chair of the Peer Review Committee and the Library's representative to the ASU West Promotion and Tenure Committee, an agenda of actions which includes:

      a.   A list of librarians undergoing mandatory review (2nd or 4th year probationary review, conditional review, or 6th year promotion and continuing appointment review)

      b.   A list of librarians undergoing non-mandatory review.

C. **External Letters**

1. Candidates for Promotion and Continuing Appointment will forward their list of six proposed external reviewers to the Dean of the Library who, in consultation with the candidate's supervisor(s) will also select six external reviewers. A final roster of six names shall include three names selected by the candidate and three names selected by the Dean.

   External letters are part of the evaluation of a librarian's records of service contributions and professional contributions (including publications) as well as position effectiveness. While ASU West Librarians cannot serve as external reviewers, external reviewers may be any of the following: (1) ASU faculty; (2) colleagues in other libraries; (3) other professional colleagues. Packets sent to external reviewers should contain a curriculum vitae at the minimum, and, if a librarian chooses, (1) a two page personal statement, and (2) no more than three documents/publications chosen by the candidate.

2. Letters from external reviewers shall be solicited by the Dean of the Library and kept on file in that office. (APPENDIX B)

D. **Review Packet**

1. Disposition of Packets:

   a. Each candidate prepares one packet for review by the Peer Review Committee. No additional copies of the packet may be made (except as noted in II.D.1.c): therefore, all members of the Committee (including academic professionals from the ASU Main libraries) review the packet which is the kept in the Library Administration office.

   b. In reviewing the packet, the committee retains the original content and order of documents in the packet as submitted by the candidate. Before the unit committee forwards the packet to the Dean of the Library, the candidate may review the non-confidential sections of the packet to insure that documents are in the order in which they were originally submitted.

   c. The Dean of the Library shall forward the review packet to Academic Affairs and may make one copy of the file for the Library's personnel file.

2. Review Packet Contents:

   This section must be used in conjunction with the ASU West document on probationary/promotion & tenure files distributed annually by Academic Affairs. The document will provide detail not outlined here, including the order of materials.

a.   The Librarian undergoing review provides:

(1)   Current Curriculum Vita (see Appendix A - Vita Template)

(2)   Personal Statement (two pages) outlining professional goals and integrating position effectiveness, professional contributions and service activities.

(3)   Position Effectiveness Section. The candidate may include the following:

(a)   Position Effectiveness Statement (two pages) See criteria for position effectiveness in the section, *Criteria and Standards for the Award of Rank and Continuing Appointment.*.

(b)   List of Internal Publications

(c)   Up to six (6) samples of internal publications

(4)   Professional Contribution Section.

(a)   Professional Contribution Statement (two pages) See criteria for professional contributions in the section, *Criteria and Standards for the Award of Rank and Continuing Appointment.*.

(b)   Up to four (4) samples of publications, creative works, and/or current working papers representing achievements.

(5)   Service Section.

(a)   Service Statement (two pages) summarizing and analyzing the three (3) service activities most descriptive of contributions is this area.

(b)   Up to two (2) samples representing achievements.

(6)   Solicited Documentation. These qualifications apply:

(a)   Any of the reviewing committees or administrators may request additional information or documentation in keeping with campus guidelines.

(b)   The Dean of the Library will serve as the liaison to obtain additional information/documentation requested from the candidate.

(c)   The information/documentation requested and received at any level will remain in the packet for the duration of the review.

b. In cases where the Supervisor oversees 75% or more of the candidate's work, the Supervisor inserts:

    (1) Supervisor's letter of recommendation which discusses position effectiveness, professional contribution and service and is based upon the standards described in the section, *Criteria and Standards for the Award of Rank and Continuing Appointment.*

c. The Peer Review Committee inserts:

    (1) The Committee's letter of recommendation which discusses position effectiveness, professional contribution and service and is based upon the standards described in the section, *Criteria and Standards for the Award of Rank and Continuing Appointment..*

    (2) A transmittal memo which documents the vote and the recommendation.

d. The Dean of the Library inserts:

    (1) A personnel action form provided by the Office of the Vice Provost for Academic Personnel.

    (2) External letters of review

    (3) The Dean of the Library's letter of recommendation which discusses position effectiveness, professional contribution and service and is based upon the standards described in the section, *Criteria and Standards for the Award of Rank and Continuing Appointment..*

E. Recommendations

1. Peer Review Committee

a. The Committee will consider the candidate's file, the letters of external review, and the supervisor(s) letter(s) where appropriate in formulating its recommendations. An official vote will be taken. The Committee will forward the file, including the Committee's recommendations to the Dean of the Library by the dates specified in the Schedule of Personnel Action published each academic year.

    (1) The report regarding a candidate undergoing promotion and continuing appointment review will include an overall recommendation for promotion and continuing appointment.

    (2) The report regarding a candidate undergoing probationary review will include recommendations on changes/ improvements or committee concerns about the candidate as necessary, plus an overall recommendation on retention.

(3)   The report regarding a candidate undergoing promotion and continuing appointment review prior to the mandatory time will include an overall recommendation for promotion and continuing appointment. A negative or split decision will also contain recommendations on changes/improvements or committee concerns about the candidate as necessary, plus an overall recommendation on retention.

(4)   The report regarding a candidate undergoing promotion review will include an overall recommendation on promotion. Should a negative or split decision occur, committee membership concerns will be addressed and recommendations for changes/improvements will be provided.

b.   The letter of recommendation from the Peer Review Committee will be accompanied by a transmittal memo which documents the recommendation and the vote.

2.   Dean of the Library

a.   The Dean of the Library will inform the candidates of the recommendations, with reasons, of both the Peer Review Committee and the Dean of the Library. These qualifications apply.

(1)   Promotion and/or Continuing Appointment candidates will be informed at least 3 working days prior to the date the review packet is due to Academic Affairs.

(2)   Candidates undergoing non-mandatory review shall have 2 working days, after being informed by the Dean of the Library of the Committee's and the Dean's recommendations, to notify the Dean that their application is (1) withdrawn, or (2) to be forwarded to Academic Affairs for the ASU West Promotion and Tenure Committee.

b.   The Dean of the Library will forward all review files to Academic Affairs.

3.   ASU West Promotion and Tenure Committee

a.   Recommendations of this Committee are forwarded to the Vice Provost for Academic Personnel.

b.   Candidate files are retained in the Office of the Vice Provost for Academic Personnel.

4.   Vice Provost for Academic Personnel.

a.   Recommendations of the Vice Provost for Academic Personnel are forwarded to the Provost.

Arizona State University West

5.   Provost

        a.   The Provost notifies the candidate and the Dean of the Library of the final decision.

III. Grievance Procedures

A.   A candidate may pursue a grievance in accordance with *ACDW Manual, Grievance Policies and Procedures for Faculty and Academic Professionals.*

Criteria and Standards for the Award of Rank and Continuing Appointment

All members of the academic professional staff in the ASU West Library are assigned a rank. Those ranks signifying librarians' eligibility for Continuing Appointment are: Assistant Librarian; Associate Librarian; and Librarian. Rank is independent of job title or function. Rank is intended to indicate professional standing and to provide a qualitative rationale for promotion.

Librarians should apply for promotion when they can provide evidence of a sustained record of performance consistent with the standards of the rank sought. Promotion must be sought concurrent with Continuing Appointment if the librarian is at the Assistant Librarian rank. A librarian holding probationary status must apply for Continuing Appointment no later than the sixth year of employment.

A.   Standards for Appointment

Minimum requirement for appointment as a librarian is a master's degree from a program accredited by the American Library Association.

The Position Announcement and Letter of Appointment will state additional position requirements.

B.   Standards for Award of or Promotion to Rank

1.   Assistant Librarian

To be appointed Assistant Librarian the individual must possess the potential to:

- Practice librarianship; and
- Participate in and contribute to a variety of professional activities; and
- Meet service responsibilities primarily within, but not limited to the Library.

Retention during the probationary period at this rank requires evidence of progress towards meeting the standards for Associate Librarian.

Continuing Appointment will not be awarded at the Assistant Librarian rank.

2. **Associate Librarian**

To be appointed or promoted to Associate Librarian the individual must exhibit evidence of a substantial extension of the record on which the award of Assistant Librarian was based and/or have sustained a record of performance and achievement as follows:

- The practice of librarianship which demonstrates mastery of one's assignment; and
- Professional contributions, completed or in progress, in which career direction is evident and which demonstrate impact on librarianship or other academic disciplines, but not to the exclusion of librarianship; and
- Significant service involvement both within and outside the Library beyond mere affiliation and attendance.

Retention during probationary period at this rank requires evidence of progress towards meeting the standards for Librarian.

Award of Continuing Appointment requires the candidate to demonstrate excellent performance and the promise of continued excellence at a level consistent with the Associate Librarian rank.

3. **Librarian**

To be appointed or promoted to Librarian, the individual must exhibit evidence of a substantial extension of the record on which the award of Associate Librarian was based and/or have sustained a record of performance and achievement as follows:

- The practice of librarianship demonstrating mastery of one's assignment and leadership within one's organization; and
- Professional contributions, including publications, which are of significance to librarianship or another academic audience; which demonstrate creativity through original thinking, research, investigation, or alternative approaches to problems and practices; and which serve to establish or enhance the reputation of both the institution and the individual beyond the local campus; and
- Leadership or established reputation in multiple service roles.

Award of Continuing Appointment requires the candidate to demonstrate excellent performance and the promise of continued excellence at a level consistent with the Librarian rank.

C. Criteria

Librarians will be judged on 3 criteria:

1) Position Effectiveness;
2) Professional Contributions; and
3) Service.

Candidates must provide qualitative and quantitative evidence of excellence in these areas to support applications for both Continuing Appointment and Promotion.

1. Position Effectiveness

Position Effectiveness is performance in the candidate's assigned responsibilities.

Standards for Performance include:

- Effective and continuous accomplishments which relate to the missions of the University and the Library, and which may include support of curricular and research efforts of the institution; interpretation of the bibliographic structure of information, literatures and disciplines; access to information; development of Library collections; application of professional standards, guidelines and protocols; and administration and management of collections, Library services and operations
- Effective accommodation of change in the position or environment in which the individual has worked during the period under review
- Contributions to organizational goals and objectives
- Innovation and creativity in professional practices
- Continuing growth in one's position and professional expertise
- Application of effective team strategies
- Application of professional standards and practices
- Knowledge and application of professional standards, guidelines and protocols

Appropriate evidence includes or might be taken from:

- Activity reports
- Administrative documents in the form of reports, handbooks, manuals, etc.
- Annual goals-based evaluations
- Application of training, course work, degrees earned and in progress, or other professional development activities
- Departmental logs and minutes
- Description of programs or projects in progress
- Evaluations by colleagues both within and outside the Library
- Exhibits

- Feedback from clients or colleagues outside the Library
- Formal evaluations of teaching by students, faculty or peers
- Innovations
- Internal Publications
- Library Committees
- Library Task Forces
- Materials produced to analyze and report Library services and operations
- Materials produced to meet Library program and service goals
- Orientation and instructional materials developed
- Program/project/proposal evaluations and summaries and other practice-related materials
- Projects or programs that demonstrate knowledge, awareness, and application of current professional trends, practices, and developments
- Recognition of expertise in assigned duties by individuals outside the Library
- Reports on or products resulting from projects at the department or Library level
- Statistical reports
- Teaching and testing materials developed
- Transcripts or other evidence of formal education activities
- Workshops Conducted

2. **Professional Contributions**

For academic librarians, scholarship consists of activities that impact and advance both the practice and science of librarianship. Such activities accomplish the exchange of information, professional practice and research findings, and may take place in workshops, seminars, meetings of professional organizations, and publications. Therefore, a candidate's contributions through any of these instruments can be considered equally legitimate elements of scholarship and professional contributions.

Similar activities within other academic disciplines also constitute professional contributions, and may be undertaken in addition to but not to the exclusion of professional contributions in the discipline of library science.

Standards for Performance include:

- Demonstration of one's professional expertise
- Leadership roles
- Recognition beyond the local campus in terms of the substance of the activity and its impact on a professional audience
- Relevance to one's position and to the development or augmentation of expertise

Appropriate evidence includes or might be taken from:

- Contributions to or authorship of unpublished professional or scholarly works that are broadly distributed
- Consulting in areas of professional expertise
- Copies of programs for seminars, workshops or other events in which one participated
- Description of works in progress
- Editorial activity--membership on editorial boards or project-based responsibility
- Elective or appointive position held in state, regional or national professional or scholarly organizations
- Evaluations of products or activities
- External letters outlining responsibilities and accomplishments
- Grants and grant proposals
- Fellowships, awards and honors received
- Leadership and application of professional expertise in the planning and implementation of professional or scholarly workshops, seminars, conferences
- Panelist or respondent in a program to a professional or scholarly audience
- Papers and poster sessions presented at programs of national, regional or local organizations
- Products of committee work
- Publications--articles, chapters, reports, books, media productions, software, bibliographies, databases, indices, critical reviews
- Published proceedings
- Proposals and leadership in their implementation which result in substantive innovations in professional practice or delivery of library services that extend outside the workplace, present new ideas or incorporate research

   Indicate whether the contribution is refereed, non-refereed, or invited where appropriate.

3.   **Service**

   Librarians holding continuing or probationary appointments are expected to actively serve the institution and the profession through the donation of time and professional expertise. Professional service to the community may also be considered.

Standards for Performance include:

To the Library:
- Activities that contribute to the shared governance of the Library
- Professional mentoring

To the institution:
- Collegial contributions that further the goals or accomplish the work of the institution

To the profession:
- Contributions of benefit to professional organizations and to other libraries

To the community:
- Exercise of one's professional competence in enhancing the image of the university or representing the university to the public

Appropriate evidence includes or might be taken from:

- Activity reports
- Committee or task force work within the institution
- Description of tasks in progress
- Elected or appointed posts in community projects or boards
- External letters outlining responsibilities and accomplishments
- Governance or consultative responsibilities within the Library or institution
- Logistical roles in professional organizations and meetings
- Outline of memberships and committee assignments
- Minutes of meetings
- Position in which one represents the University or Library
- Products of committee work
- Program announcements of workshops, seminars, conferences
- Published proceedings
- Volunteer work

Appendix A

Curriculum Vitae Template

Arizona State University West

NAME
Curriculum Vitae
Date

WORK
Address
Telephone
Fax

EDUCATION (Most recent first)

Year	Institution	Degree

PROFESSIONAL CREDENTIALS OR CERTIFICATIONS

ACADEMIC AWARDS/HONORS/FELLOWSHIPS (Most recent first)

Year	Title	Awarding Institution

EMPLOYMENT (Most recent first)

Month Year-Year	Position/Title	Institution/Place

CREDIT COURSES (Taught or developed)

POSITION EFFECTIVENESS AND PROGRAM IMPROVEMENT

Innovations
Library Committees
Library Task Forces
Internal Publications
Workshops Conducted

PROFESSIONAL CONTRIBUTIONS

Committees (Professional Contribution-others under service) {Most current first}

National
Association/Organization, Committee, Year

Regional
Association/Organization, Committee, Year

State
Association/Organization, Committee, Year

52 - Public Institutions

Local
Association/Organization, Committee, Year

Elected/Appointed Offices (Specify which) [Most current first]

Editorial Research Boards/Editorships/Juries

Presentations (Most current first)

Oral Presentations/Papers
Title of Presentation; Conference/Workshop; Date

Poster Sessions
Title of Presentation; Conference/Workshop; Date

Panels
Title of Presentation; Conference/Workshop; Date

Grants

Internal (Title of funded proposal; Name of principal investigator; Type of grant; Institution; Dollar amount awarded; Date)

External (Title of funded proposal; Name of principal investigator; granting agency, foundation, or institution; Dollar amount awarded; Date)

Pending/Unfunded (Optional)

Publications

Refereed Journal Articles (Most recent first)
Author(s), Year of pub., Title of article, Name of Journal, Vol., No., Pages

Non-Refereed Journal Articles (Most recent first)
Author(s), Year of Pub., Title of Article, Name of Journal, Vol., No., Pages

Books
Author(s), Year of Pub., Title of Book, Place of Publication, Publisher

Chapters in Books
Author(s), Year of Pub., Title of Chapter, Name(s) of Editor, Title of Book, Pages, Place of Publication, Publisher

Completed Manuscripts Accepted For Publication

Refereed Journal Articles (Most recent first)
Author(s), Year of pub., Title of article, Name of Journal, Vol., No., Pages

Non-Refereed Journal Articles (Most recent first)
Author(s), Year of Pub., Title of Article, Name of Journal, Vol., No., Pages

Books

Author(s), Year of Pub., <u>Title of Book</u>, Place of Publication, Publisher

<u>Chapters in Books</u>
Author(s), Year of Pub., Title of Chapter, Name(s) of Editor, <u>Title of Book</u>, Pages, Place of Publication, Publisher

Manuscripts Under Review
Author(s), Title of Article, <u>Name of Journal</u>, Current Status

Research (Or Manuscripts) in Progress

Book Reviews

Abstracts

Published Proceedings

Contributions to Newsletter/Columns

Unpublished Manuscripts (Optional)

> Articles
> Books
> Chapters
> Bibliographies

PROFESSIONAL DEVELOPMENT

Memberships

Conferences/Workshops (Most current five years or ASU West plus selected highlights)
[Most current first]
Year   Workshop/Conference Title   Month

Other (Continuing Education Courses/Credits)

SERVICE

<u>Profession</u>
Association/Organization, Committee/Office (Elected/Appointed), Date

<u>Community</u>
Association/Organization, Committee/Office, Date

<u>University</u>
Committee/Office (Elected/Appointed), Date

<u>Campus</u>
Association/Organization, Committee, Year

Appendix B

Letter to External Reviewers

Date

Name
Address

Dear

_____ is being considered for _____ [Continuing Appointment and promotion to Associate or Full Librarian] as a member of the Academic Professional Staff at Arizona State University West. As part of our review procedure, we request external reviews of the candidate's professional performance, professional contributions and service.

To this end, we ask that you evaluate _____'s effectiveness as a librarian in regards to any of the criteria below. Your appraisal of the significance and impact of _____'s performance should address both quality and quantity. We also ask that you indicate the extent and nature of your acquaintance with the candidate. A current vita is enclosed to assist you in this process.

Our continuing appointment and promotion decisions are based on the candidate's record of accomplishment in the areas of:

> 1. Librarianship, which is the candidate's professional expertise in the areas of _____. This requires mastery in the areas of assignment, fulfillment of duties associated with the position, contribution to organizational goals and objectives, innovation and creativity in professional practices, and development of professional expertise.

> 2. Professional Contributions, which are activities that demonstrate one's expertise and participation in the profession. Some examples of appropriate activities might include: elected or appointed positions in state, regional or national professional or scholarly organizations; publications or productions of a professional or scholarly nature; presentation of papers to a professional or scholarly audience and similar accomplishments and contributions.

> 3. Service, which includes contributions to the university, profession and community. Some examples of appropriate activities might include: elected or appointed positions; committee assignments within the institution; governance or consulting responsibilities within the Library, institution, or community and similar accomplishments and contributions.

We solicit external letters of evaluation on a confidential basis. Your name was selected by Academic Affairs from a suggested list provided by either the candidate or the Dean of the Library. Under our procedures, neither your name nor the content of your letter will be shared with the candidate. Only the personnel committees and academic administrators legitimately involved in promotion and continuing appointment {tenure} decisions will view your letter. We take the greatest care to insure confidentiality.

I thank you for taking the time to form a professional judgment as to the professional standing which has been achieved by _____. If you could respond within 30 days, it would be most helpful. If you are unable to meet this timeline or find yourself unable to provide an evaluation for any reason, please write or call me at your earliest convenience. Thank you in advance for your assistance.

Appendix C

PRC Recommendation & Evaluation Templates

Probationary Review - Committee Recommendation

Probationary Review - Committee Evaluation

Promotion and Continuing Appointment - Committee Recommendation

Promotion and Continuing Appointment - Committee Evaluation

(To be completed on ASU West Library letterhead stationery)

DATE: *(Insert appropriate date)*

TO: Helen Gater
             Dean of the Library

FROM: Library Peer Review Committee
             Librarian, Chair *(insert names of Committee members)*
             Librarian
             Librarian
             Librarian
             Librarian

RE: _____ *(insert as appropriate 2nd year, 4th year, Conditional)* Probationary Review
             of _____ *(insert Librarian's name)*.

The Library Peer Review Committee met to review the _____ *(insert as appropriate 2nd year, 4th year, Conditional)* probationary file of _____ *(insert Librarian's name)* with the following recommendation. The Committee voted _____ to _____ *(insert committee vote)* to recommend /not recommend *(select one)* retention of _____ *(insert Librarian's name)*. Attached is the Committee's letter of recommendation.

Arizona State University West

ASUW Library Peer Review Committee Evaluation

_____ (*insert Librarian's name*): _____ (*insert as appropriate 2nd year, 4th year, Conditional*) Probationary Review

Date (*Insert Appropriate date*)

_____ (*insert Librarian's name*) had _____ years (*insert number of years*) of library experience prior to coming to ASU West. In addition to her/his (*select one*) library degree, _____ (*insert Librarian's name*) has a _____ (*insert additional degrees held*). While this review takes into account her/his (*select one*) relevant previous experience, the comments contained here primarily address accomplishments while at ASU West. The ASU West Library Peer Review Committee recommends/does not recommend (*select one*) retention and submits the following evaluation of her/his (*select one*) work.

Position Effectiveness

Professional Contributions

Service

Summary

(To be completed on ASU West Library letterhead stationery)

DATE: (*Insert appropriate date*)

TO: Helen Gater
               Dean of the Library

FROM: Library Peer Review Committee
               Librarian, Chair (*insert names of Committee members*)
               Librarian
               Librarian
               Librarian
               Librarian

RE: Promotion and Continuing Appointment Review of _____ (*insert
               Librarian's name*)

The ASU West Library Peer Review Committee met to review the promotion and continuing
appointment file of _____ (*insert Librarian's name*) with the following
recommendation. The Committee voted _____ to _____ (*insert committee vote*) to support /not
support (*select one*) the application for promotion and continuing appointment. Attached is the
Committee's letter of recommendation.

Arizona State University West

ASUW Library Peer Review Committee Evaluation

_____ (*insert Librarian's name*): **Promotion and Continuing Appointment Review**

Date (*Insert Appropriate date*)

_____ (*insert Librarian's name*) had _____ years (*insert number of years*) of library experience prior to coming to ASU West. In addition to her/his (*select one*) library degree, _____ (*insert Librarian's name*) has a _____ (*insert additional degrees held*). While this review takes into account her/his (*select one*) relevant previous experience, the comments contained here primarily address accomplishments while at ASU West. The ASU West Library Peer Review Committee supports/does not support (*select one*) the application for promotion to Associate Librarian with the award of Continuing Appointment/Full Librarian (*select one*) and submits the following evaluation of her/his (*select one*) work.

Position Effectiveness

Professional Contributions

Service

Summary

Appendix D

Schedules

ASU West Academic Affairs:
Schedule of Personnel Actions, Faculty and Academic Professionals

ASU West Library:
Schedule of Personnel Actions

ASU West Library:
Calendar of Scheduled Reviews

State University of New York College at Plattsburgh

Approved: March 29, 1996
Amended and Approved: September 13, 1996

ELABORATIONS ON PERFORMANCE REVIEW OF THE
LIBRARY FACULTY

Table of Contents

I. Academic Librarianship: A Context

II. Criteria for Performance Reviews

III. Guidelines for Application of Criteria for Reappointment

IV. Guidelines for Application of Criteria for Promotion

V. Guidelines for Application of Criteria for Continuing Appointment

VI. Procedures for Performance Review

VII. Guidelines for Performance Review File Preparation

I. Academic Librarianship: A Context

The goal of the Feinberg Library is to support the instructional, research, and public service mission of the college through the design of user-centered programs. Librarians play a key role in achieving this goal and their activities have a direct bearing on the quality of undergraduate and graduate education. The work of academic librarians is varied and specialized. It is organized around the categories of collection development, bibliographic organization, interpretation of the collection, and access to information. New information technologies are changing the methods used to carry out these traditional functions and causing a shift of emphasis in libraries. The focus is changing from building large local collections to improving access to materials both inside and outside the library through local networking, automation, and the internet. Academic librarians provide the expertise needed to shape a responsive library in a changing environment and to develop the wider range of services the library offers the college community. Librarian participation in faculty governance and academic planning on all levels ensures a successful transition to a new information environment while maintaining a commitment to the Library's presence as an intellectual center of the campus.

Although academic librarians have a variety of individual responsibilities related to the organization and management of library functions, they share in a set of core responsibilities. These may include activities in such areas as collection development, information services, library instruction programs, and team or group management structures. Core responsibilities in collection development involve liaison responsibilities to particular departments; in information services they include reference assistance, and in instruction they consist of teaching sections of Library 101. In addition, all librarians participate in programmatic groups that are responsible for a variety of management, planning, and implementation issues. New technologies and automation require greater knowledge of current developments in librarianship and information science, as well as collaboration and sharing of responsibilities that cross traditional organizational divisions. The text below describes the main programmatic areas of the library and the intellectual dimensions of these areas.

A. <u>Collection Development</u>: The selection and acquisition of materials to meet the intellectual needs of the college community is the traditional foundation upon which the library has been built. The selection process is a fundamental responsibility of librarians and depends on a series of intelligent choices made within the context of local academic needs, priorities, and goals. Librarians involved in collection development need to develop a thorough knowledge of the curriculum and research requirements of departments, as well as an understanding of the processes of scholarship and scholarly communication. Collection Development needs to be coordinated in an orderly and structured manner to ensure a rational acquisitions process and that library resources are expended equitably and effectively. Collection analyses and evaluations need to be coordinated and conducted periodically to determine quality, usage, and budgetary adequacy.

B. Resource Access and Delivery: An unorganized set of materials without a system for user access can hardly be called a library collection, no matter how well it has been selected. In cataloging, catalog maintenance, and the other numerous operations that create systems for ready access to the collection, expertise is needed to ensure that all materials, regardless of format, are organized by appropriate schema, classifications, and groupings. This expertise is especially important as libraries continue to move into electronic, networked environments, replacing manual files with automated systems that integrate operations such as cataloging, acquisitions, and serials control. In addition, librarians with responsibility in this area play a leading role in providing users with new forms of rapid access to information through document delivery programs, electronic interlibrary loan, and photocopy services.

C. Information Systems: The rapid growth of automated library systems and the need to create a fully integrated electronic information environment require librarian expertise in the planning, development, and implementation stages. Defining the future relationship between local automated library systems and remote sites, networks, and bibliographic utilities such as OCLC depends heavily on the knowledge of librarians in this area. Maintaining the technical infrastructure, providing the oversight for installed systems, and projecting future growth and the replacement of hardware/software are major activities of librarians involved with systems. These librarian responsibilities are essential if users are to take advantage of new research options made available by the latest information technologies.

D. Information Services: Organized groups of materials, whether available locally, in remote databases, or on the Internet, are of limited value without qualified academic personnel who can help identify them, assist with their use, and teach others how to find, evaluate, and use them. Librarians engaged in reference services provide the interpretive link between an information problem, its analysis, and ultimate solution. This ability to translate problems into the terms that point to an answer helps connect users with appropriate parts of the library's collection and introduces them to the world of information beyond the library's walls. Librarians with reference expertise make intelligible for users an information environment that is constantly expanding and that utilizes network services to uncover on-site as well as remote resources.

E. Instructional Services: Librarians engaged in instructional services are crucial to the process of fostering independent and intelligent use of library resources, search and retrieval systems, and networks. Their activities are essential if users are to develop a critical understanding of how the products of research are to be evaluated. Librarians teach when analyzing problems at an information desk, producing guides for users, providing formal library instruction, or helping users adapt to new forms of electronic access. Librarians play a crucial role in improving intellectual access to information.

F. Patron Services: Easy physical access to local collections through borrowing privileges and services that provide direct instructional support, such as media distribution and reserve operations, all enhance the user's ability to acquire information. Library privileges allowing access to collections and services must be clearly articulated and communicated to the diverse group of patrons that an academic library serves. Librarians are responsible for creating an environment for users that encourages serious study, makes people comfortable asking questions and using services, and promotes self-sufficiency. As automated systems and networking allow libraries to provide ready information on the availability of materials to users both locally and at remote locations, it is essential that Patron Services develop the structures and organization for efficient use of local materials and those acquired through resource sharing. Librarians in Patron Services play a crucial role in integrating new information technologies into existing services through knowledgeable use of networks, automation, and effective communication with library users.

G. Special Collections: Most libraries place materials unique in form and content in separate collections. These materials often require a special approach to their selection, organization, interpretation and access. Collection development, for example, focuses on local and regional materials, and the administration of college archives. Knowledge of special library methods for preserving, conserving, and organizing these unique materials plays an important role in creating the conditions for public access. Equally important is the ability to interpret the unique place of these materials in the college curriculum and their value to the community, and to provide instruction in their use. Librarian expertise is critical in developing the policies to strike a balance between preservation requirements and the needs for public access.

The combination of individual responsibilities, core responsibilities, shared activities, and general faculty commitments needs to be kept in mind during the evaluation process so that a librarian can be evaluated on the basis of her or his total contribution to the library and the college.

II. Criteria for Performance Reviews

The criteria for evaluation from the Policies of the Board of Trustees and Performance Reviews of Academic Employees: Policies and Procedures have been enhanced to reflect the contributions of librarians, whose contributions differ in kind and emphasis from those of traditional teaching faculty. Librarians have a twelve month contractual obligation to provide library service. Librarians' contributions to the profession must be judged on a variety of individual and cooperative achievements. Library service, rather than classroom instruction or research and publications, must be the primary factor in evaluating librarians' contributions to the college's mission.

The criteria are to be used as a basis when evaluating librarians for reappointment, promotion and continuing appointment. It is not intended that each library faculty member meet all the representative measures given below, but only those most relevant to the individual's contributions as a librarian and to the responsibilities required of that individual by the library.

1. CRITERIA

a) <u>Mastery of Subject Matter</u>--as demonstrated by such things as advanced degrees, licenses, honors, fellowships, scholarships or awards, or reputation in the field of librarianship.

Librarians also may demonstrate mastery of subject matter in another subject field(s) by such things as advanced degrees, licenses, honors, fellowships, scholarships or awards, or reputation in the subject matter field.

b) <u>Effectiveness of Teaching</u>--as demonstrated by such things as development of classroom teaching materials; development of guides, publications, training programs or workshops; work at the Reference Desk; professional consultations; and student/patron reaction, as determined from evaluation documents, surveys or interviews, or observation of public reference work.

c) <u>Effectiveness in Librarianship and Scholarly Ability</u>--with the expansion of the criterion for scholarly ability to reflect the Boyer principles, much of a librarian's work previously defined as professional effectiveness now falls into the category of scholarly ability.

This criterion is demonstrated by such things as success in developing, carrying out or providing library services or group projects; performing significant research in the field of librarianship and contributing to the profession of librarianship through publications or presentations to professional organizations; providing professional consultation; or reputations among colleagues.

Effectiveness as a librarian requires an understanding of the various operations and services of the library and the ability to interpret and integrate them, identify and analyze problem areas, offer constructive suggestions and promote satisfactory solutions.

It also requires the ability to communicate and cooperate effectively with library staff, library and other faculty, students and administrators in advancing the priorities and fulfilling the objectives of the library, its programmatic groups, its Division, and the college.

d) <u>Effectiveness of University Service</u>--as demonstrated by such things as college, University, public service, committee work, administrative work and work with students or community in addition to formal teacher-student relationships.

e) <u>Continuing Growth</u>--as demonstrated by such things as reading, research, attendance at or participation in professional organizations, conferences, workshops or other formal activities to keep abreast of current developments in librarianship; and being able to handle successfully increased responsibility, including demonstration of creativity and initiative in the accomplishment of professional responsibilities.

Examples of continuing growth may include work towards or completion of additional advanced degrees, graduate courses, attendance at professional workshops and conferences.

III. Guidelines for Application of Criteria for Reappointment

Candidates for reappointment in rank are expected to meet the criteria for that rank as noted below.

IV. Guidelines for Application of Criteria for Promotion in Rank

The representative measures below indicate the type and level of accomplishment desirable in the various ranks. These measures are guidelines for evaluating candidates for promotion to specific ranks. Candidates should use the measures as a guide and not as a checklist of prescribed goals.

All ranks require a Master's degree in Library Science from an accredited school. This degree is defined as an A.L.A. accredited degree, a pre-1948 American or Canadian BLS, a Fellow of the Library Association of Great Britain or other library and information science degrees from any country as long as the awarding institution has been accredited by the appropriate association or agencies. We support the following statement on the Terminal Professional Degree for Academic Librarians: "The Master's degree in library science from a library school accredited by the American Library Association is the appropriate terminal professional degree for academic librarians." (Approved as policy by the Board of Directors of the Association of College and Research Libraries, a division of the American Library Association, on January 23, 1975.)

A. Assistant Librarian

This is the initial appointment level and requires no previous professional experience. Appointment at this rank is based on the academic record and references associated with earning the Master's degree from an ALA accredited program and potential for professional development.

This is not a tenurable rank, although time spent in this rank shall accumulate towards tenure.

State University of New York College at Plattsburgh

B. Senior Assistant Librarian

1. <u>Mastery of Subject Matter</u>: Demonstrates solid background in library and information services through intelligent application of this background to core responsibilities.

2. <u>Effectiveness of Teaching</u>: Demonstrates strong performance of core responsibilities of teaching and reference through a description of one's own teaching style/philosophy, summary of students' evaluations, samples of assignments and/or student work, guides and peer evaluation of reference desk activities.

3. <u>Effectiveness in Librarianship and Scholarly Ability</u>: Demonstrates strong performance of core responsibility of group work and in areas of expertise or unit facilitation, through qualified peer evaluation; demonstrates evidence of initiative and creativity in these activities; contributes to the library and librarianship through special projects, grant activity, presentations or publications, provides library services directly or through facilitation of library unit(s).

4. <u>Effectiveness of University Service</u>: Assumes collegial responsibilities by service to college, university or community.

5. <u>Continuing Growth</u>: Contributes to the library and librarianship through reading, research, attendance at professional conferences, workshops related to improvement of librarianship; keeps abreast of current developments in core areas of responsibility and/or special area of expertise; demonstrates willingness to accept increased responsibility.

C. Associate Librarian

1. <u>Mastery of Subject Matter</u>: Demonstrates significant mastery of library and information services through receipt of local honors, awards, reputation in this field. It may be supplemented by demonstration of mastery of other subject areas.

2. <u>Effectiveness of Teaching</u>: Demonstrates significant, strong performance of core responsibilities of teaching and reference through a description of one's teaching style/philosophy, summary of students' evaluations, samples of assignments and/or student work, guides, classroom materials and peer evaluation of reference desk activities.

3. <u>Effectiveness in Librarianship and Scholarly Ability</u>: Demonstrates significant, strong performance of core responsibility of group work and in areas of expertise or unit facilitation through qualified peer evaluation; demonstrates significant initiative and creativity in these responsibilities and ability to assume increased responsibility in core areas or areas of specialization/facilitation; continues and expands contributions to library and librarianship through special projects, grant awards or publication in regional or state publications, including development of electronic access tools.

4. Effectiveness of University Service: Demonstrates significant, strong service to the college, university or community.

5. Continuing Growth: Contributes significantly to the library and librarianship through demonstration of research projects, participation in professional conferences and/or contributions to growth of self and colleagues in core areas of responsibility and/or special area of expertise; demonstrates ability to assume increased responsibility.

D. Librarian

1. Mastery of Subject Matter: Demonstrates superior mastery of library and information services through receipt of state or national honors and awards; demonstrates reputation in field beyond the regional level and/or completes additional advanced degree in appropriate field. This may be supplemented by demonstration of mastery of other subject areas.

2. Effectiveness of Teaching: Demonstrates superior performance in core responsibilities of teaching and reference through a description of one's teaching style/philosophy, summary of students' evaluations, samples of assignments and/or student work, guides, classroom materials and peer evaluation of reference desk activities.

3. Effectiveness in Librarianship and Scholarly Ability: Demonstrates superior performance of core responsibility of group work and in areas of expertise or unit facilitation through qualified peer evaluation; demonstrates excellence through leadership and/or completion of new programmatic initiatives; excellence in ability to carry out increased responsibility in core areas or area of specialization/facilitation; demonstration of evidence in excellence in contributions to library and librarianship through significant special projects, grant awards, electronic access tools, or publications beyond the state level.

4. Effectiveness of University Service: Demonstrates leadership in service to college, university or community.

5. Continuing Growth: Makes major contributions to the library and librarianship through demonstration of superior performance in research projects; leadership in professional organizations and/or major contributions to growth of self and colleagues in core areas of responsibility and/or area of expertise; demonstrated leadership in areas of increased responsibility.

E. Distinguished Librarian

The process for promotion to the Distinguished Librarian rank follows policies, procedures, practices, and guidelines promulgated by the Chancellor of the State

State University of New York College at Plattsburgh

University of New York, and provisions, if any, in the Agreement Between UUP and the State of New York.

Details on this rank are available on the SUNYLA gopher.

V. Guidelines for Application of Criteria for Continuing Appointment

The criteria for continuing appointment (tenure) are closely allied to the criteria for promotion in academic rank. The relationship between tenure and rank shall be the same for library faculty as for other faculty in the institution.

VI. Procedures for Performance Review

A. Library Performance Review Schedule and Process[1].
    1. Librarians up for reappointment , continuing appointment, or promotion shall submit their Review File to the Dean of Library and Information Services according to the schedule set forth in the annual campus Performance Review Calendar[2].
    2. The Library Peer Review Group shall meet one or more times to form a recommendation on each individual under performance review.

B. Appeal Process
    Individuals may initiate the Optional Review Procedure (except for promotion for Librarian) outlined in the Performance Reviews of Academic Employees[3] Agreement (Article III.12.1 - III.12.6).

VII. Guidelines for Performance Review File Preparation

1. The individual's Review File should reflect a fair, comprehensive, clearly arranged and organized representation of accomplishments and performance.

Refer to the Performance Review of Library Faculty[4] for an elaboration of academic criteria, and to the Performance Reviews of Academic Employees agreement. (Articles V.1 - V.1.7) for specific file preparation guidelines.

Consult the documents listed below for complete, official details on timing, requirements and rights of all concerned.

---

[1] Current Agreement between UUP and the State of New York (Articles 30, 31, 32)

[2] Annual memo from the Presidents. "Performance Review Calendar."

[3] "Performance Reviews of Academic Employees: Policies and Procedures: (1995 Agreement)

[4] :Elaborations on Performance Review of Library Faculty" Feinberg Library

Private Institutions

Alfred University
Alfred, New York

Eckerd College
Saint Petersburg, Florida

Saint Olaf College
Northfield, Minnesota

HERRICK LIBRARY FACULTY PROMOTION AND TENURE POLICY/PROCEDURE STATEMENT

The Herrick Library faculty endorse the Standards for Faculty Status for College and University Librarians as adopted by the membership of the Association of College and Research Libraries. In keeping with these standards which call for librarians to "form as a library faculty whose role and authority is similar to that of the faculties of a college, or the faculty of a school or a department," the following policies and procedures have been adopted by the Herrick Library faculty.

1.   The evaluation process for promotion and tenure will begin on August 1st of each year. On this date all P&T documentation will be due to the chairperson of the P&T committee, with a copy to the University Librarian. Each librarian will be expected to submit the following information:

   a) An updated c.v. (including academic degrees, awards, committee service, publications, etc.)
   b) Faculty activity report for the previous year
   c) Planning document for the previous year with outcomes
   d) Planning document for the current year
   e) Copies of any relevant creative and scholarly activity
   f) A self-evaluation (from all librarians under consideration for tenure or promotion -- optional for all others)
   g) Peer reviews for all colleagues being evaluated for tenure forecast, tenure, tenure review, or promotion (Handbook for Faculty, Administrative Staff and Technical Specialists, p.19,20)
   h) Additional relevant information is desirable, especially from librarians being evaluated in the 4 categories listed in #7. Although not required, letters from colleagues (on and/or off campus), library support staff or others who can speak knowledgeably to the performance of the librarian being evaluated, are very useful.

2.   All untenured library faculty will be reviewed annually (tenure forecast). All tenured faculty will be subject to tenure review on five year multiples of the anniversary of granting tenure (e.g. a library faculty member who initially received tenure in 1984 would be reviewed in 1989, 1994 etc.)

3.   All peer reviews need to address the criteria for promotion and tenure as elaborated in "Evaluation of Herrick Library Academic Faculty for Promotion and Tenure". Addressing these criteria in the same order that they occur in the document greatly facilitates the work of the P&T committee and is strongly encouraged.

4.   Librarians will prepare their information packets for the P&T committee to be self-presenting. In other academic units of the University, Division Chairpersons present faculty members' documentation to their respective P&T committees. Since this level of administration is not present in Herrick Library's organization, librarians may either invite another librarian to assist them in preparation and presentation of their packets or undertake it themselves.

5.   The next step will be a review of the materials by the P&T committee, followed by a meeting with the University Librarian for clarification. After this meeting the P&T committee members will meet by themselves to formulate a recommendation to the University Librarian and the Provost. This recommendation will be submitted to the University Librarian and the Provost by December 15.

6.   In evaluating library faculty members, the P&T committee will give greatest weight to criterion 1: Effectiveness as a Librarian. Heavy weight will be given to criterion 2: Contributions to the Advancement of the Profession. Criterion 3: University Service, will be examined to determine if the person being evaluated is a contributing member of the University community.

7.   The University Librarian will forward her recommendation directly to the Provost. The Provost will then present his recommendation to the President.

8.   The Provost will report the President's decision to the University Librarian, who will, in turn, inform the candidate of the outcome of the process. Outcomes will be made known to all faculty no later than February 15th.

9.   Sabbatical leave requests must also be presented to the P&T committee for consideration. Requests should clearly define the objectives and expected outcomes for the leave. Only tenured candidates with 6 years of service are eligible to apply. A plan for meeting the responsibilities of the librarian who would be on sabbatical, while not strictly necessary for the committee, would be a useful exercise prior to making the application.

10.   Individual evaluation conferences with the University Librarian will take place each spring. Any documentation submitted to the P&T Committee during that academic year may be discussed. Any problems, current or potential, should be raised at this time. Plans for the next year will also be discussed to ensure agreement in focus between the library faculty and the University Librarian.

11.   The Handbook for Faculty, Administrative Staff and Technical Specialists, revised 8/86, contains a general outline of the P&T process for the University as a whole. In that outline the issues of promotion in rank are addressed. Promotions from Assistant librarian to Associate librarian and from Associate librarian to (full) Librarian are not automatic. Outstanding performance, "Interest and active participation" in Library and University affairs, demonstrated contributions to the advancement of the profession, "contribution to the development and welfare of the greater community served by the University" are required of those being considered for this recognition.

Application for advancement in rank may be made by the individual librarian, the University librarian, or the Provost. Application for (full) librarian rank (Professor) may be made after 5 years of service have been completed following the year in which tenure was granted.

12.   This statement is subject to annual review.

EVALUATION OF HERRICK LIBRARY ACADEMIC FACULTY FOR
PROMOTION AND TENURE

INTRODUCTION

The academic faculty of Herrick Memorial Library shares the
University's goals of pursuing, achieving and maintaining academic
intellectual excellence. Progress towards these goals requires a
faculty of librarians of high professional and academic caliber,
supported by adequate collections and facilities.

By defining librarians as academic faculty, Alfred University
recognizes that librarians make a fundamental intellectual contribution
to the educational, research, and public service missions of the
University.

While the criteria by which librarians are judged must relate to the
general criteria applied to all academic faculty, they must also relate
to the unique role of librarians in the academic community. Members of
the Herrick Library faculty are expected to demonstrate excellence,
primarily in their contributions to the library system and its users.
Professional and creative activities which focus on a variety of
individual and cooperative achievements are another demonstration of
excellence.

CRITERIA FOR PROMOTION AND TENURE

1. Effectiveness as a Librarian

   This is the most important criterion by which librarians are
   judged. No accomplishment in the other criteria, however
   impressive, may compensate for a deficiency here. Effectiveness
   as a librarian shall be interpreted to mean the successful
   application of knowledge of library materials, procedures,
   bibliographic and management techniques to developing and
   organizing the library collection, interpreting the library
   collection for its users and facilitating use of library services
   and resources.

   In evaluating "Effectiveness as a Librarian" some factors for
   judging the quality of performance are innovation, initiative,
   consistency, dependability, accuracy, ability to work effectively
   with others, oral and written skills, and professional attitude.
   In order to maintain a high level of effectiveness in
   librarianship, a librarian must also demonstrate continuing
   professional growth and development. Since the master's degree in
   library science is the terminal professional degree for practicing
   librarians, there are two methods of professional development,
   which are not mutually exclusive:

   Formal Education

   Formal education consists of enrollment in courses leading to

1

a degree or certificate. Examples of formal education goals
are a second master's degree or doctorate in a subject field,
certificate programs, course work selected to improve the
librarians' skills.

Continuing Education

Continuing education usually consists of participation in
workshops, seminars, training sessions etc. designed to help
the librarian keep current in areas of specialty or to
develop new skills or competencies.

Herrick librarians are involved in and must be effective in one or
more of a variety of specific functions within the library. They
are as follows:

a.   Bibliographical Control of the Collection

This involves the application of a knowledge of bibliographic
organization, including cataloging and classification
principles, to monographs, serials, documents and other
library materials so that these materials are effectively
organized for use, and so that the information contained in
them is fully represented and maintained in the card catalog
and other bibliographic records of the library. Of
particular concern is the ability to analyze library
materials, define their bibliographic components and describe
them systematically in terms that will be meaningful to
users. The effective analysis of library materials requires
a continuing awareness of changing areas of knowledge and may
also involve specialized linguistics and/or subject expertise
as appropriate. This also includes a continuing critical
appraisal of bibliographic services and innovations and the
adaptation of these to meet user needs.

Library faculty performing some of these functions may
include archivists, catalog maintenance librarians,
catalogers, documents librarians, special collections
librarians, serials librarians.

b.   Development of Collections

This involves the responsibility of selection, acquisition
and preservation of materials which support the intellectual
life of the University. Effective performance in this area
requires a thorough knowledge of new and retrospective
publications in all formats in subject fields, familiarity
with the University's instructional and research programs,
continual awareness of trends in curricula and research, and
an ability to evaluate the merits and suitability of
individual publications with respect to the University's
programs. It also requires a thorough knowledge of trade,
scholarly, and national bibliographies, current publishing
trends, domestic and foreign book trades and the ability to

2

apply this knowledge accurately in developing and using efficient methods to acquire and preserve materials for the library's collections.

Library faculty performing some of these functions may include acquisitions librarians, collection development librarians, archivists, bibliographers, documents librarians, special collections librarians, serials librarians, reference librarians.

c. Reference, Information and Instructional Service

This involves substantial knowledge of print and online reference and information sources in specific areas as well as a general knowledge of the broad areas of the humanities, social sciences, sciences, nursing, or business and their literatures. The ability to apply effectively this knowledge ins assisting library users is essential. Teaching effectiveness in a variety of situations, such as individual consultations, orientation sessions, and classroom lectures or formal courses in bibliography and research methodology is of particular importance. Compilation of bibliographic guides and other materials to enhance user access to information is also important.

Categories of library faculty performing some of these functions may include bibliographers, computer search service analysts, interlibrary loan librarians, library instruction librarians, serials librarians, reference librarians, special collections librarians.

d. Administration and Management

This involves the administration and management of library operations in areas which require academic knowledge and judgment. Important factors to consider include leadership, development of unit objectives in the context of goals and objectives of the Library and the University, planning and implementation of objectives through the identification of problems and alternative solutions, effective management of resources and personnel, and improvement of communication at all levels.

Categories of library faculty performing some of these functions may include department heads, coordinators and other library administrators.

2. Contributions to the Advancement of the Profession

Involvement in activities relevant to the advancement of or sharing of knowledge in librarianship help to broaden a librarian's ability to function effectively as a member of the library faculty. The evaluation of activities relevant to the advancement of the profession should focus primarily on

3

qualitative factors such as intellectual rigor and clear evidence of the ability to support the teaching and research mission of the University. Creativity, innovation and sound scholarship are especially valued. Participation in professional activities on local, state, regional or national levels should be evident.

3. University Service

Involvement in the governance structure of the Library and the University increases the librarian's awareness of the inter-relationships of units on the campus. It also gives the librarians an opportunity to contribute to the direction and development of the Library and the University. This generally takes the form of effective participation in committees and task forces. Activities may also include participation in ad hoc Library and University groups or community organizations. Evaluation of University Service shall focus primarily on qualitative factors. Among the factors to be considered for effective participation are: fulfillment of basic obligations of attendance, relevant and timely contributions to proceedings, working relations with other members, chair responsibilities.

GUIDELINES FOR APPLICATION OF CRITERIA FOR PROMOTION IN RANK

Academic rank reflects professional growth and achievement in the areas of 1. Effectiveness as a Librarian, 2. Contributions to the Advancement of the Profession, and 3. University Service. At all levels, effectiveness as a librarian is of primary importance. Continuing education activities are also expected at all ranks.

Assistant Librarian

Appointment at or promotion to the rank of Assistant Librarian requires evidence of increasing effectiveness as a librarian coupled with a record of contributions to the advancement of the profession, and service to the University.

Associate Librarian

Appointment at or promotion to the rank of Associate Librarian requires evidence of sustained effectiveness as a librarian, substantial professional contribution to the institution, as well as the attainment of a high level in bibliographical activities, in research, or in other professional endeavors.

Librarian

Appointment at or promotion to the rank of Librarian requires evidence of outstanding effectiveness as a librarian. Significant and sustained contributions to the profession and the University must be evident. Contributions both to the Library and profession are at the highest level and demonstrate a keen awareness of issues facing the library profession and higher education. The record should give clear and

4

strong support that continuing growth and first-rank performance as a librarian has been demonstrated and will continue.

GUIDELINES FOR APPLICATION OF CRITERIA FOR TENURE

Persons granted tenure must have fulfilled criterion 1 -"Effectiveness as a Librarian" - in an outstanding manner. They must show evidence of professional activities of high quality in the areas of "Contributions to the Advancement of the Profession" and/or "University Service" and must also show evidence that such contributions will continue.

10/89 bylawpt

Alfred University

Herrick Library Evaluation

Date:
Evaluator:
Evaluatee:

1. Effectiveness as a Librarian:
    Innovation

    Initiative

    Consistency

    Dependability.

    Accuracy

    Ability to work effectively with others

    Oral and written skills

    Professional attitude

Continuing professional growth and development

Specific Professional Functions:
a. Bibliographic control of the collection
   Ability to analyze library materials, define bibliographic components and describe them systematically in terms that will be meaningful to users

   Awareness of changing areas of knowledge

   Appraisal and adaptation of bibliographic services and innovations to meet user needs

b. Development of Collections
   Knowledge of new and retrospective publications in subject fields

   Familiarity with the University's instructional and research programs

   Awareness of trends in curricula and research

   Ability to evaluate the merits and suitability of individual publications with respect to the University's programs

c. Reference, Information and Instructional Service
Knowledge of print and online reference and information sources

Ability to apply knowledge effectively in assisting library users

Teaching effectiveness

Quality of library guides and other instructional material

d. Administration and Management
Leadership

Development of unit objectives in the context of goals and objectives of the Library and the University

Planning and implementation of objectives through the identification of problems and alternative solutions

Effective management of resources and personnel

Improvement of communication at all levels

2. Contributions to the Advancement of the Profession
   Creativity

   Innovation

   Scholarship

   Participation in professional activities

3. University Service
   Participation in committees and task forces

   Attendance

   Relevant and timely contributions to proceedings

   Working relations with other members

   Chair responsibilities

Eckerd College

FACULTY

Guidelines for Promotion in Rank

1. Criteria used in evaluating recommendations for promotion are the same as those used when considering faculty for tenure. These criteria are spelled out on pages 6-3 through 6-5 in the *Personnel Policies Manual*. It is assumed that favorable promotion recommendations made after a faculty member is tenured will be based on an assessment of continued excellence in academic instruction, mentorship, professional productivity and college and community service. While growth and development in all criteria will be assessed, excellence in teaching and mentoring will be the minimum requirements for promotion.

2. Teaching faculty and professional librarians who have not earned the terminal degree in their fields will ordinarily be hired initially with the rank of Instructor. Upon completion of requirements for the terminal degree, they will be eligible for promotion to the rank of Assistant Professor.

3. Promotions from the rank of Assistant to Associate Professor will ordinarily not be made until after a faculty member or professional librarian has been awarded tenure. To be eligible for promotion in rank to Associate Professor, a person will ordinarily have completed a minimum of six years of full time teaching or professional librarianship (three years of which must be at Eckerd College). If a person is not promoted to the rank of Associate Professor by the end of the tenth year of full time service, the Academic Standards Committee will review the case annually and communicate to the person the reasons why a favorable promotion recommendation has not been made.

    When considering promotion to Associate Professor, the Committee will expect evidence that the person has (1) developed as an effective teacher and mentor, (2) assumed an increasingly influential role on campus in the development of a learning community, (3) demonstrated professional activity in his/her field, and (4) started to develop a professional reputation beyond the College.

    a. In exceptional cases, the Committee will receive nominations for promotion to Associate Professor for colleagues who are not yet due a tenure decision. Such nominations should speak to both (1) the merits of the case for promotion and (2) the reasons for the exceptional timing.
    b. The Committee may recommend to the President that tenure and promotion to Associate Professor occur at the same time in cases where the individual under consideration has met the evaluation criteria listed above in an exceptional manner.

4. Promotion from the rank of Associate Professor to Professor will not be considered until a person has held the rank of Associate Professor for a minimum of three years. If a person is not promoted to Professor by the end of the tenth year as an Associate Professor, the Academic Standards Committee will review the case annually and communicate to the person the reasons why a favorable promotion recommendation has not been made.

    When considering promotion to Professor, the Committee will expect sustained evidence that the person has (1) continued to develop as an effective teacher and mentor, (2) assumed an influential role on campus in the development of a learning community, (3) kept professionally active in his/her field, and developed a professional reputation beyond the College.

Examples of Professional Productivity

Examples of professional productivity are publications and/or art exhibits, recitals, theatrical productions etc., as appropriate; presentations at professional meetings; presentations in one's area of professional competence to the general public; leadership in professional associations; attendance at professional meetings; grants/fellowships; grant proposals; new or revised academic programs; college approved consultantships; participation in funded research projects; honorary or invited professorships/artist-in-residencies.

Professional productivity is to be distinguished from college and community service, which includes service on college committees and to college organizations, administrative duties, participation in community and religious organizations, and assisting other faculty.

,Suggested Questions for Use in Formulating Annual Statements of Professional Goals

The following questions are intended to provide guidance to faculty in writing annual statements of professional goals. They are not intended to be exhaustive nor is a response to every one of them required; however, it is hoped that these questions will help faculty to focus and express the formulation of their goals in a way that will be most useful to them and to those who are expected to review and comment on them.

Instruction

1. What courses will you be repeating?
2. What courses will be new?
3. What contributions will you make to the general education program and the major?
4. To what kinds of instructional methods will you be giving particular attention?
5. What plans do you have for reenforcing or strengthening your teaching skills?
6. What kinds of learning do you plan for your students to achieve?
7. How do you plan to use the information from your past course evaluations in planning for your teaching this year?
8. If you are planning to teach at Eckerd College in addition to your work in the undergraduate residential program, what do you plan to be doing (PEL, Leadership Academy, summer term, etc.)?
9. What are your longer range goals (beyond this year) for course development and the strengthening of your teaching skills?

Mentorship

1. How many associates do you expect to have?
2. What do you expect to be the areas in which your associates will most need assistance and guidance?
3. What methods will you use to meet these needs?
4. What will be the evidence for assessing the effectiveness of your mentoring of this year's group of associates?
5. What are your longer range goals (beyond this year) as a mentor?

Professional Productivity

1. What specific plans do you have for keeping abreast of current developments in your discipline?
2. What specific plans do you have for contributing in a scholarly or artistic way to your discipline?

Eckerd College

3.   What specific things do you plan to do in the way of presentations, consultations or other outside work that accrue as the result of your professional competence?
4.   What longer range plans (beyond this year) do you have for your professional development and for making contributions to your discipline?
5.   In what ways do you expect students to benefit from your professional productivity?

College and Community Service

1.   What specific responsibilities have you agreed to assume or activities do you plan to undertake to serve the campus community; e.g., committee service, administrative responsibility, advising student organizations, special services to Special Programs?
2.   What specific responsibilities have you agreed to assume or activities do you plan to undertake to serve the community beyond the campus; e.g., the church, social agencies, civic organizations, businesses?
3.   What are your longer range goals (beyond this year) in the area of on-campus and off-campus community service?

Faculty Evaluation Schedule

Sept. 30:   Faculty send annual activity reports (self-evaluations for the previous year and statements of professional goals for the current year) to collegial chairs (librarians to library director).

-    Self-evaluations will include the extent to which goals have been achieved and reasons for major successes/shortcomings.

-    Professional goals will address both short term (coming year) and long term objectives.

-    Evaluations and goals will include instruction, mentorship, professional productivity, and college and community service (including plans/outcomes of leaves).

-    See "Suggested Questions for Use in Formulating Annual Statements of Professional Goals," page 2-10.

Oct. 1:   Peer evaluators and collegial chairs begin evaluation of untenured faculty, using an agreed upon common format, and begin visits to classes. Tenured discipline colleagues are also encouraged to submit comments.

Peer evaluators and collegial chairs visit classes of tenured faculty every three years, and peer evaluators write evaluations of tenured faculty every three years, coinciding with the Academic Standards Committee review of tenured faculty.

Oct. 15:   Collegial chairs/library director send faculty annual activity reports to the Dean of Faculty, along with their comments. Comments are also sent to faculty, who may meet with chairs to discuss their evaluation.

Oct. 30:   Dean of Faculty sends faculty members written responses to their annual activity reports. Faculty are encouraged to respond in writing to any questions raised by the Dean and may meet with the Dean to discuss their evaluations.

Feb. 10:   Faculty due tenure and promotion decisions submit interim annual activity reports to the Dean of Faculty and collegial chairs.

Peer evaluators and collegial chairs send their reviews of faculty due <u>tenure</u> and <u>promotion decisions</u> to the Dean of Faculty.

April: Registrar distributes <u>Mentor Evaluation</u> forms to all students. Mentor Evaluations are kept on file in the Dean of Faculty's office.

June 1: Peer evaluators send written evaluations of <u>untenured</u> faculty (including instruction, mentorship, professional productivity, college and community service) and any suggestions for improvement, to the Dean of Faculty with copies to collegial chairs and faculty being evaluated. Faculty may submit written responses to evaluations, and may meet with peer evaluators to discuss their evaluations.

ECKERD COLLEGE	*Personnel Policies & Procedures*	Page 6-3
		Academic Freedom and Tenure
		Adopted April 23, 1982
		Revised

THE ROLE OF TENURE AT ECKERD COLLEGE - (Continued)

If the tenure system is to function well in achieving its broad goals of academic excellence, it is imperative that all parties concerned understand the basis on which tenure decisions will be made. Not only do such criteria specify the institution's definition of professional excellence, but also they serve to help define the continuing obligation of a tenured faculty member to the institution. In the absence of specified criteria, tenure decisions could be made on an idiosyncratic and constantly shifting basis, to the possible detriment of the individual and the interests of the College. The burden of proof of excellence properly falls on the probationary faculty member. As such, it is not unreasonable to expect such faculty members to evidence foresight and ingenuity in providing measurable indices of professional excellence.

C. Criteria for Awarding Academic Tenure

1. Academic tenure may be awarded only to faculty members whose primary responsibility to the College lies in a teaching function, and to full-time professional librarians who hold faculty status. Teaching faculty and librarians will be evaluated according to the same criteria, except that it is recognized that the nature and scope of the librarian's teaching and mentoring functions are necessarily different from those of the classroom teacher.

Academic tenure is awarded to support and enhance the teaching effectiveness of the institution's faculty. As conceived by the College, the concept of effective teaching embraces not only traditional effectiveness in the classroom setting, but also the ability to help guide the intellectual development of students through academic counseling and personal example. It includes, moreover, the maintenance of a program of personal scholarship, through which a faculty member remains an active contributor to his/her field of inquiry and thereby brings to his/her teaching the excitement of scholastic or artistic creativity.

ECKERD COLLEGE	*Personnel Policies & Procedures*	Page 6-4
		Academic Freedom and Tenure
		Adopted April 23, 1982
		Revised

THE ROLE OF TENURE AT ECKERD COLLEGE - (Continued)

While it is expected that individuals will vary in the way in which they approach their teaching, counseling, and scholarship responsibilities, it is possible to specify a common body of institutional expectations against which all faculty members will be evaluated.

a. Academic Instruction - The faculty member is expected to devote himself/herself energetically to the mastery of the material which he/she teaches, to maintain rigorous intellectual standards for himself/herself and his/her students, to strive for clarity and effectiveness in his/her teaching methodology, and to serve as a model of intellectual honesty and academic achievement.

b. Mentorship - The faculty member is expected to achieve a high level of effectiveness in the academic counseling of students. This means that the faculty member will achieve competencies in one-to-one faculty-student relationships, maintain a thorough grasp of the total College program and the individual needs of his/her students and take responsibility for helping students to correct academic deficiencies through referral to appropriate College services.

c. Professional Productivity - The faculty member is expected to develop and maintain a program of research, primary scholarship, or artistic production as appropriate to his/her discipline. The products of such activity may be public in the form of papers, books, professional presentations, plays, exhibitions, etc., or they may be manifest primarily through enhanced teaching effectiveness on the part of the faculty member.

d. College Service - The faculty member is expected to contribute to the College by serving on the College's committee structure. Service to the College may include, but not be limited to, any of the following: (1) serving as Collegial Chair, (2) serving as discipline coordinator, (3) serving on standing or ad hoc committees, and (4) serving as faculty advisor to student organizations.

ECKERD COLLEGE	*Personnel Policies & Procedures*	Page 6-5
		Academic Freedom and Tenure
		Adopted April 23, 1982
		Revised

THE ROLE OF TENURE AT ECKERD COLLEGE - (Continued)

The foregoing constitute satisfactory criteria. Faculty members will, in addition, be evaluated on their ability to work with and command the respect of students and colleagues and their commitment to the goals and purposes of the institution.

Since affirmative tenure decisions commit the College to long-term and costly obligations, factors other than the individual's competencies may enter into the decision. Among others, these include the long-term projected enrollments in the individual's area of specialty, the number of other tenured faculty members in related areas, and program priorities of the institution.

3. Insofar as tenure is a mechanism specifically designed to enhance the quality of teaching and scholarship, tenured faculty members who assume permanent administrative duties occupying more than half their defined commitment to the College will be expected to surrender their academic tenure at the end of three years.

Fairness requires that the faculty members on probationary status at the present date should be given time as needed to adjust their activities and efforts to insure a reasonable chance of receiving a favorable tenure decision. The following implementation policy is therefore adopted:

D. Formation of a Faculty Committee on Academic Standards

In accepting tenure, a faculty member receives a number of significant benefits, including greatly heightened job security, enhanced guarantees of academic freedom, and an institutional presumption of his/her academic excellence. At the same time, however, the faculty member assumes the obligation to the institution to maintain the high standards of scholarship, teaching, and community service for which he/she received tenure initially. While research interests or teaching methodologies may shift with time, and the visibility and vigor with which a faculty member carries out his/her work may change with increasing age and intellectual maturity, the commitment to excellence in teaching and scholarship must remain. Tenure must not shield faculty members who fail to meet these obligations.

4-15

5. A faculty member who does not have a terminal appointment and who is not recommended for reappointment, upon request shall be given an explanation of the action in an informal conference with the department chair or the Dean of the College and, again upon request, shall be given a statement of reasons in writing.

IX. Tenure

After the expiration of a probationary period, and after an affirmative tenure decision has been made, members of the faculty of St. Olaf College shall have tenure (that is, assurance of continuous employment by the College), and they shall be dismissed or their service terminated only for adequate cause and with due process except in the case of retirement for age.

Faculty members with tenure recognize that tenure conveys both privileges and responsibilities. They will regard themselves as a part of that group of faculty members who, because of the continuing relationships to the institution which their tenure involves, share responsibility for the total life and program of the institution. They will resign from their positions only after careful consideration of the effect upon the work of the College and only after ascertaining that the College is in a position to continue in a competent manner the work for which they have been responsible.

1. The award of tenure shall always be based on an explicit judgment by the College. Tenure shall not be acquired by default through the mere passage of time in the probationary period. During the probationary period an explicit decision concerning the granting of tenure shall be made for each faculty member, who shall be notified in writing of this decision. Notice must be given before September 1st of the final year of the probationary period.

2. The probationary period of faculty members who hold academic rank will commence upon the first tenure-track appointment and shall not exceed seven years of full-time equivalency. [For exception in instructor rank, see paragraph 4 below.] Service at other institutions of higher education or in prior years at St. Olaf shall be counted on the basis of the following conditions, and shall be stated in the first letter of standard appointment:
    a. The probationary period for any faculty member initially appointed to the rank of associate or full professor shall not exceed three years.
    b. All service, up to a maximum of three years , at the rank of instructor or above at another institution of higher education may be counted for those initially appointed as full-time instructors or assistant professors. The decision concerning the number of years to be counted shall be negotiated between the faculty member and the College during the first year of service at St. Olaf and shall be confirmed in writing in a letter from the Dean of the College to the faculty member before September 15 of the second year of service at St. Olaf.
    c. Prior service at St. Olaf in a term or terminal appointment may be counted towards the probationary period, with a maximum of three years full-time equivalency. The decision concerning the number of years to be counted shall be negotiated between the faculty member and the College at the time of the initial tenure-track appointment.

3. An individual receiving a terminal appointment before September 1st of the academic year in which a tenure review would be held is not automatically guaranteed tenure review.

4. A teacher with the rank of instructor may continue to serve in that rank beyond the seventh year and without tenure, provided such a relationship is agreeable to both St. Olaf College and the individual.

5. The following basic requirements are necessary conditions for tenure:

   a. All candidates must have demonstrated that they meet high standards of professional competence in their disciplines and that they possess the ability and interest to ensure continued growth.

   b. Except under unusual circumstances, all candidates must have attained a terminal degree in their disciplines (or equivalent professional distinction).

   c. All candidates must have either a tenure-track full-time appointment or a tenure-track part-time appointment to be eligible for tenure review.

6. All tenure decisions shall be made according to the Procedures for Granting Tenure and Promotion.

7. Constraint is necessary in granting of tenure in order that St. Olaf College secure the best possible personnel to serve its program. Such constraint is to be observed by all participants in the process of awarding tenure.

8. Tenure decisions shall be based on judgments in the following two areas, listed in descending order or priority:

   a. The candidate's qualifications as measured by the Standards for Faculty Evaluation.
   b. Considerations of personnel needs within the candidate's department (e.g., areas of specialization, unusual teaching styles, retirement plans, number of tenured persons) as they relate to the Department's Staffing Plan.

9. Any previous experience shall be considered insofar as it contributes to effectiveness in the specified criteria.

10. Granting tenure does not imply promotion; however, a person may be considered simultaneously for tenure and promotion.

X. Promotion in Rank

1. The purpose of promotion is to recognize effective teaching, research, scholarship, creative activity, and contributions to the College.

2. The academic ranks of the College for its faculty shall be as follows:

   a. Instructor
   b. Assistant Professor
   c. Associate Professor
   d. Professor

3. The College uses the designation "Distinguished Lecturer," "Visiting Lecturer," or "Visiting Professor" to identify persons appointed to the faculty, usually on a temporary basis, to whom the college policies of promotion, tenure, and rank do not apply.

SIGNIFICANT PROFESSIONAL ACTIVITY - LIBRARY FACULTY

The Faculty Manual states the importance of scholarly and creative activity as a grounding for teaching. It also states that "the college gives primary emphasis to effective undergraduate teaching." Paraphrasing this, the librarians value scholarly and creative activity, but give primary emphasis to filling the responsibilities of their positions on the College library faculty. The demands of these positions differ from those placed on most position to position. Additional significant professional activity can be expected to reflect this diversity.

Formal teaching may require physical presence in the classroom for six to nine hours a week, and perhaps as many hours devoted to advising, help sessions, and labs. The remainder of a teachers duties may be scheduled more flexibly. In contrast, the librarians' work schedule has usually been a forty hour week in the library, since their work is closely involved with the staff, the collections, and users. It is difficult to spend much of the time on other significant professional activity. Moreover, librarians, like department chairs, have certain administrative functions, and scheduling allowances are made in recognition of this. They have ten or (for the College Librarian, Systems Librarian and Archivist) eleven month schedules which allow a catch-up period in the summer.

In the absence of more flexible scheduling and large blocks of time conductive to research (except during sabbaticals), the librarians believe that their additional professional activities should usually be given less weight than is the case with classroom teachers. They should be pursued only to the extent that they do not interfere with primary responsibilities.

Librarians differ from other faculty in more than their work schedule. The field of library/archival science is not exactly comparable to disciplines such as history or physics. The terminal degree is the master's, following an undergraduate degree with a major in some "subject" area. Academic librarians usually couple their training and expertise in library/archival science with a strong interest and academic background in another discipline. Therefore, it may be as appropriate for librarians to pursue graduate study in one of these disciplines, to do creative work in them, and to participate in their professional associations, as to carry out these activities in library/archival science.

The St. Olaf librarians have agreed upon the following list of additional significant professional activities, which should be given more weight when considering promotion to associate and full professor. The two areas of activity listed under category I are of equal importance. Although the categories are listed in descending order of importance, they are relative and there may be some overlap.

Rolvaag Memorial Library
1510 St. Olaf Ave.
Northfield, MN 55057-1097

I. PUBLICATIONS, UNPUBLISHED WORKS, ORAL PRESENTATIONS AND CREATIVE WORK OR PERFORMANCE such as: that relating directly to library science or disciplines related to the librarian's duties. Evaluation will be based on the jurying provided by the publisher or, in the case of unpublished works, internal or external evaluators.

ACTIVITY IN PROFESSIONAL ORGANIZATIONS BEYOND THAT NORMALLY EXPECTED OF MEMBERS, such as: leadership roles which contribute significantly to policy decisions or programs, at the national, regional and state level. Evaluation will be based on the scope and scale of work involved, as demonstrated to internal or external evaluators.

II. ADDITIONAL STUDY OR TRAINING beyond the normal in-service workshops or seminars required by the librarian's position, as for a supplemental advanced degree in library science or in another academic discipline.

III. HONORS, AWARDS AND GRANTS
    1. From external sources.
    2. Refereed by St. Olaf or another employer.

RATIONALE

The two categories comprising level one in this statement provide substantial, different, benefits. Publications, oral presentations, and other types of creative endeavor may enhance the reputation of the faculty member, the department, and the College. Ideally this activity will also improve job performance by renewing interests and broadening knowledge. The amount of research or other effort required by an oral presentation or creative work may equal to that demanded by many kinds of publication, so that they should be accorded the same relative weight.

Involvement in professional organizations in a capacity which influences the experience or performance of others possesses many of the same benefits as publication. It has the advantage (which it shares with oral presentations and other types of personal contact) of providing for the immediate exchange of ideas. Among librarians it has additional importance because of the pressing needs of systems networking, national and international standards, and the speed with which technological changes take place. Professional organizations fill a major role in setting priorities and standards, as well as disseminating information.

Section II. reflects the fact that the master's degree in library science is the terminal degree in the field. (In the case of the Archivist, the terminal degree may be either a master's degree in history, augmented by courses in archival methods, or a master's degree in library science with a concentration in archives.) Further graduate study, or some sort of technical training, may be valuable to librarians, depending upon the individual situation. This study may be in library and information science, or it may be in some academic discipline, development, reference, etc.

Approved by the Librarians 9/27/89; Subsequently passed by Review and Planning Committee

Document Involving Unions

Trenton State College
Trenton, New Jersey

TRENTON STATE COLLEGE
Roscoe L. West Library

TENURE GUIDELINES FOR LIBRARIANS

Tenure commits the College to an individual for decades. It is awarded only when the candidate presents a strong record on all criteria. When there is doubt about a candidate, s/he will not be tenured.

At Trenton State College, as at many other colleges and universities across the country, tenure criteria have been changed and made more rigorous in recent years. It cannot be assumed that because a librarian achieved tenure in the past, another librarian with a comparable record of performance will achieve it now or in the future. It is no longer the case, if it ever was, that every basically competent librarian who logs the requisite number of years of service will probably be tenured.

It must be remembered that the recommendation of the Library committee charged with reviewing tenure applications is **advisory** to the Dean, whose recommendation is **advisory** to the Council of Deans, whose recommendation is **advisory** to the Vice-President for Academic Affairs, whose recommendation is **advisory** to the President, whose recommendation is **advisory** to the Board of Trustees. The Board makes the final decision. These tenure criteria have been drafted by the Dean of the Library in consultation with the Assistant Deans and the Council of Deans, both of which have approved them, and have also been approved by the Vice-President for Academic Affairs and, implicitly, by the higher College administration.

It should be noted that the State Colleges' contract with the AFT prohibits requiring librarians to have a second graduate degree (i.e., beyond the ALA-accredited Master's) in order to get tenure. However, a second graduate degree in a subject area related to the librarian's position should greatly enhance his/her reference, collection development, amd user education work, expertise in research and scholarship, and credibility as a faculty member.

"Related" would include, for example, any of the following degrees for a Business and Economics Librarian: a doctorate in librarianship/information science; an MBA or MPA; or a Master's or doctorate in economics, education, or business, and possibly in other subject areas such as mathematics or computer science. For an Access Services and Periodicals Librarian, related degrees would include a doctorate in librarianship/information science, an MPA or MBA, or an advanced degree in computer science or a subject area for which s/he formally took collection development responsibility.

An application for tenure will be greatly strengthened by the citation of a second graduate degree related to the candidate's position. However, it will not substitute for any of the stated requirements under categories (2) and (3) below.

Tenure criteria for librarians fall into 3 categories --- in order of emphasis:
      (1) librarianship
      (2) service to (a) the profession, (b) the Library, and
          (c) the College
      (3) research and scholarship

Although applications for tenure should cite all significant activities and accomplishments that fall into these categories, the tenure decision will be based on work that the candidate has done while at Trenton State College.

(1) **Librarianship**
      Excellence in librarianship is the _sine qua non_ for tenure. Even if a librarian demonstrates superior performance in the other two categories, tenure will not be awarded if performance as a librarian falls short of excellence.

"Excellence" transcends "competence"; it requires assertiveness, initiative, imagination, innovativeness, evaluation of results, identification of problems, devising of solutions, and continuous revision of programs and procedures as necessary. It also requires keeping up to date in the profession generally, with "state of the art" knowledge of one's own professional specialty. This knowledge should be applied to enhance the Library's services and optimize its use of available resources.

                  *   *   *   *

Criteria (2) and (3) necessitate evaluations of formal presentations and publications. The following must be borne in mind:
      (a) Degree of responsibility in co-authoring, co-editing, or co-presenting, determined partly by whether the candidate's name is the first listed on the published product, will be taken into account. Documentation of degree of responsibility may be required;
      (b) Any book cited as support for a tenure application must have been published by a reputable scholarly, professional, or commercial publisher.
      (c) "Publication" does not necessarily imply "paper." Publication may be in any format: paper, microform, CD-ROM, online, etc.
      (d) Only formal conference proceedings constitute publication of presentations. "Formal" publication indicates publication for broad professional distribution, reviewing, and sale. Gatherings of camera-ready papers for limited distribution are not considered formal publications.
      (e) Length and approach of a publication or presentation will be taken into account when judging its substantiality.
      (f) Distinctions between "refereed" and "nonrefereed" journals, and between "professional" and "research or scholarly" contributions are crucial. See discussions of these differences below in section (3).

* * * *

(2) **Service**

(a) The Profession

A record of substantial contribution to the profession, outside of Trenton State College, is required for tenure. A substantial record would comprise, at minimum: at least two major contributions, or (b) at least one major contribution plus two or more minor contributions, or (c) a number of minor contributions which add up to a significant record. It should be the goal of every candidate to exceed the minimum. Documentation of the candidate's specific accomplishments (e.g., while serving as President of a professional association) may be required. Meeting the minimum letter of the requirement may not correspond to adequately fulfilling it if there was not a substantial, verifiable, contribution.

Major contributions include:

Holding an elected major office (i.e., Board member, President, Secretary, or Treasurer) in a significant international-, national-, or state-level professional association: e.g., the Association of College and Research Libraries; New Jersey Library Association; the Music library Association; Beta Phi Mu;

Holding an elected Presidency, directorship, chairship, or Board membership of a significant regional or local professional association: e.g., Central Jersey Library Cooperative;

Holding an elected chairship of a subdivision of a significant international-, national-, or state-level professional association: e.g., one of the divisions or Round Tables of ALA;

Serving as editor, or as a member of an active editorial board, of an international- or national-level professional periodical or publication series: e.g., any journal or publication series sponsored by an ALA division or by another international- or national-level professional association;

Authoring or co-authoring a professional book or textbook, a substantial article for a professional periodical, or a substantial chapter for a professional book;

Editing or co-editing a professional book or textbook;

Authoring or co-authoring a series of short articles in an international- or national-level professional periodical;

Delivering a major professional speech or paper at an international- or national-level conference: e.g., a keynote speech or sole speech at a major program at an ALA conference --- if there is associated publication;

Authoring or co-authoring a successful proposal for a major grant;

Creating, or substantially contributing to the development of, an international-, national-, or state-level database, network, conference, or other electronic system or event with significant utility for the profession. Documentation of degree of responsibility may be required;

Carrying out a consultancy of major importance --- as evaluated by, among other factors, its scope and length;

Serving on a Middle States or national-level (e.g., ALA/COA) accreditation review team.

Minor activities are more various and somewhat harder to define. They include, but may not be limited to:

Holding a minor elected or appointed office in a significant professional association at any level;

Chairing, or, in some cases, serving on, an active committee of, a professional association; documentation of the committee's specific accomplishments during the candidate's service, and the candidate's degree of responsibility for the accomplishments, must be presented;

Authoring or co-authoring a substantial article for a state- or regional-level professional periodical;

Authoring or co-authoring a shorter article in an international- or national-level professional periodical, or in a professional book;

Authoring or co-authoring a substantial review article (i.e., of at least 1,500 words) in an international- or national-level professional publication;

Authoring or co-authoring a series of shorter book, media, or database reviews in an international- or national-level professional publication (e.g., Choice; RQ; Library Journal);

Authoring or co-authoring a series of shorter articles in a state- or regional-level professional periodical;

Serving as editor, or as a member of an active editorial board, of a state- or regional-level periodical or publication series;

Authoring or co-authoring a successful proposal for a small grant;

Delivering a major professional speech or paper at an international-, national-, state-, or region-level conference which is unaccompanied by formal publication. A manuscript of the paper must be provided;

Serving as a "regular" (i.e., several times) expert manuscript referee for a scholarly or professional journal or for a reputable scholarly, professional, or commercial book publisher;

Carrying out a minor consulting assignment;

Serving on an external review team of less significance than Middle States accreditation;

Presentation of a significant "poster session" at a professional conference;

In some cases, briefer presentations or local-level presentations may be considered, but they will be evaluated case by case. Usually, they will fall into the categories of "Librarianship" or "Service."

(b) To the Library/To the College
In addition to giving service to the profession, the candidate must show a strong record of service to the Library and the College --- i.e., service beyond excellent performance of his/her job. No minimum standard is set; the Dean will consult with new librarians about their service activities. However, should a librarian have questions about the adequacy of his/her

service record, s/he has the responsibility of initiating a discussion with the Dean.

Service to the Library includes:
Service on standing, ad hoc, and search committees -
-- especially as chair; documentation of the committee's specific
accomplishments during the candidate's service, and the candidate's
degree of responsibility for the accomplishments, may be required -
-- with those committees that meet frequently or have an especially
heavy workload weighing more heavily than those that do not;
A variety of other possible activities that are useful to the
Library, are optional, and fall outside the candidate's position
description: e.g., writing "This Week" book columns; creating
exhibits in the exhibit cases.

Service to the College includes:
Service on standing and advisory committees ---
especially as chair or other officer; documentation of the
committee's specific accomplishments during the candidate's
service, and the candidate's degree of responsibility for the
accomplishments, may be required --- with committees that meet
frequently or have a heavy workload (e.g., CUPPS; FIRSL) weighing
more heavily than those that do not (e.g., some of the Advisory
Committees);
Service on Faculty Senate or as an AFT chapter officer;
A variety of other possible activities that are useful,
optional, and fall outside the candidate's position description:
e.g., advising student groups; teaching the Library's independent
reading course; participating in freshman orientation week.

(3) Research and Scholarship
"Research and scholarship" may be (and, ideally, are)
professionally applicable, but they differ from "professional"
writing in that they proceed from a theoretical perspective, and
they enrich and advance knowledge.
In librarianship and information science, "research" usually
refers to new conclusions generated by the discovery of new information or the new systematization or quantification of data.
The intelligent presentation and interpretation of research is
scholarly, but "scholarship" also includes informed, thoughtful
discussion and fresh interpretation of known things and of other
writings. Thus, a thoughtful bibliographic essay that sheds new
light on the writings cited (such as is typically published in
Advances in Librarianship or in long "review articles" --- as dis-
tinct from "rviews" --- in journals such as Library Qarterly) may
be a contriution to scholarship, depending on its length, intellectual depth, and the nature of the writings cited.

To illustrate, consider the problem of recording reference
statistics. (1) A simple presentation of a recommended method (or
methods) of recording them, based on the experience of one or a few
libraries, would be a professional contribution and would not clas-

sify as research or scholarship, even if some data were presented to illustrate or support the recommendation, and even if it were published in a refereed journal. (2) A study comparing and evaluating various ways of keeping the statistics and/or comparing similar statistics-keeping methods in different libraries, etc., using sound empirical research methods, and placing the results within the context of related published studies, would classify as "research." (3) An essay citing, synthesizing, and, through thoughtful analysis, drawing fresh ideas or conclusions from all of the significant published literature on the subject, would classify as "scholarship."

Refereed Periodicals vs. Non-refereed Periodicals

Tenure-track librarians should attempt to place their articles --- especially research and scholarly articles --- in "refereed" journals. A refereed journal has external experts evaluate submitted manuscripts. Often, this evaluation is "double-blind": i.e., the manuscript author and the referee do not know one another's identity; even when it is not double-blind, the referee's identity is shielded from the author. By contrast, in an unrefereed journal, the editor(s), rather than selected external experts, decide what to publish. In an unrefereed journal, contributions may even be solicited, with publication virtually assured ahead of time.

A distinction must also be made between the refereed and unrefereed articles in a refereed journal. For example, in Library Quarterly, a refereed journal, review essays and special features (e.g., articles in the "Resources for Scholars" and "Cover Design" series) are solicited. And in Journal of Academic Librarianship, major articles are refereed, but "On My Mind" articles are not.

Requirement

To qualify for tenure, a librarian should have:

(1) authored or co-authored at least one substantial, refereed, research or scholarly article in a refereed journal; or

(2) authored or co-authored a substantial research or scholarly book, or substantial chapter in such a book, published by a reputable scholarly, professional, or commercial publisher; note that textbooks may or may not be considered "scholarly," depending upon their subject, their scope, and their level of treatment; or

(3) presented or co-presented a competitively-selected research or scholarly contribution to an international-, national-, or state-level conference, with publication of the paper or at least of its abstract in a formally published conference proceedings. (When only the abstract has been published, the manuscript should be included with the tenure application.)

Meeting the minimum letter of the requirement may not correspond to adequately fulfilling it if there was not a substantial contribution.

The subject of the publication(s) or presentation(s) must be related to the candidate's position at Trenton State College --- though this can be fairly broadly interpreted. Thus, for example, work in the fields of librarianship, education, and information science would be relevant for all librarians; but an article about economics would be relevant only to the work of the Business and Economics Librarian (unless it dealt with the economics of information, or of libraries or other nonprofit institutions!).

There are some prestigious, scholarly, nonrefereed journals and annuals in library and information science. Publication or several publications in these, combined with a strong record on the other criteria, may suffice to meet the requirement for research and scholarship.

Important Note:
A very strong record of major and minor accomplishments in the category of "Service to the Profession" --- i.e., a record that substantially exceeds the minimum requirement --- may stand in place of the "Research and Scholarship" requirement. However, this will be decided case by case, a consideration that will focus on the scope and significance of each contribution as well as on the number of contributions. No candidate should assume that any particular record of professional contributions will be adequate to exempt him/her from meeting the requirement for research and scholarship.

In all cases, if a librarian has any doubt about whether a particular activity will meet, or help meet, a requirement, s/he bears the responsibility for discussing the activity with the Dean and dispelling that doubt. Given the gravity of the decision and the commitment by the College that a positive decision entails, dubious applications for tenure will be denied even if the doubt is small.

September 1994

Evaluation Forms

Huntingdon College
Montgomery, Alabama

Wheaton College
Wheaton, Illinois

Tarleton State University
Stephenville, Texas

COMMENTARY OF THE DIRECTOR OF THE LIBRARY

Rating on a scale of 1 to 5, 1 being the highest:

_____ 1.   Informal contact with students and support of student development.

_____ 2.   Reliability as related to official duties.

_____ 3.   Ability to work professionally with others.

_____ 4.   Support of departmental work.

_____ 5.   Support of academic student activity.

_____ 6.   Availability of students for help in academic studies.

_____ 7.   Availability to other clientele for help.

_____ 8.   Scholarly attitude and professional accomplishments.

_____ 9.   Capacity for inspiration and encouragement of colleagues in scholarly and career achievements.

_____ 10.   Demonstration and conveyance of favorable image of the Library.

_____ 11.   Library skills presentation.

_____ 12.   Favorable student response.

_____ 13.   Evidence of creative thinking and problem solving ability.

_____ 14.   Ability to supervise subordinates firmly, fairly, and with guidance.

_____ 15.   General qualities.

COMMENTS:

SELF-DESCRIPTIVE COMMENTARY

This self-descriptive report is intended to help the process of improving one's professional effectiveness. A description of your OWN views on your ability as a librarian, professional accomplishments, ability to inspire students and colleagues, commitment to the Library and the College, and service to the community is necessary to insure the emergence of a complete profile.

Please five very careful consideration to each item, scoring yourself on a 1 (highest) to 5 (lowest) scale. While you should not let modesty prevent you from clarifying your greatest assets, it is just as important to be clear regarding your shortcomings.

I. Professional Ability

1. _____ Enthusiasm for and interest in librarianship.

2. _____ Organization in job performance.

3. _____ Clarity and conciseness of communication.

4. _____ Encouragement and concern for students.

5. _____ Encouragement and concern for other clientele.

6. _____ Demonstration of a comprehensive knowledge of the field.

7. _____ Active encouragement of students to seek your help.

8. _____ Do outside activities interfere with your responsibilities as a librarian? ("5" if this happens a lot, "1" is not at all.)

9. _____ Reading and research in librarianship in general.

10. _____ Reading and research in academics as related to librarianship.

11. _____ Your overall performance.

II. List and discuss any innovations that you have attempted at the College.

III.   List any factors at the College that interfere with your being a more effective librarian and faculty member.

IV.   What do you feel is your most outstanding contribution to the Library and Huntingdon College?

V.   Compared to others in your department, how would you rate your research, publications, performances, or other professional endeavors? (Please comment)

VI.   Compared to others in your department, how would you rate your contribution and commitment to college service? (Please comment)

VII.   Compared to others in your department, how would you rate your service to and involvement with the community? (Please comment)

VIII.   List any areas in which you need improvement.

INFORMAL REVIEW OF LIBRARY FACULTY

NAME _____ RANK _____

DEPARTMENT _____ EVALUATION PERIOD from _____ to _____

Job Description: _____ attached _____ under revision, will be forwarded

GENERAL

1. Possesses general knowledge beyond area of specialty:

   ___ Broad   ___ Adequate   ___ Limited

2. Possesses knowledge of specialty:

   ___ Excellent   ___ Good   ___ Fair   ___ Poor

3. Sets priorities and accomplishes important work first:

   ___ Nearly always   ___ Usually   ___ Sometimes   ___ Seldom   ___ Never

4. Demonstrates initiative:

   ___ Often   ___ Sometimes   ___ Seldom   ___ Never

5. Accepts responsibility:

   ___ Nearly always   ___ Usually   ___ Sometimes   ___ Seldom   ___ Never

6. Identifies problems and promotes their solutions:

   ___ Often   ___ Sometimes   ___ Seldom   ___ Never

7. Considers the ideas of others and alternative approaches to services and procedures:

   ___ Nearly always   ___ Usually   ___ Sometimes   ___ Seldom   ___ Never

8. Understands the various operations of the library and interprets them:

   ___ Exceptionally well   ___ Very well   ___ Satisfactorily   ___ Poorly

9. Is actively involved in furthering the objectives of the Library and the College:

   ___ Nearly always   ___ Usually   ___ Sometimes   ___ Seldom   ___ Never

10. Is familiar with the College's academic programs and can translate this knowledge into effective services:

    ___ Exceptionally well   ___ Very well   ___ Satisfactorily   ___ Poorly

7

SUPERVISORY

1. Welds staff into a unit with clearly recognized goals and objectives:

___ Exceptionally well   ___ Very well   ___ Satisfactorily   ___ Poorly

2. Is available to counsel and assist subordinates:

___ Nearly always   ___ Usually   ___ Sometimes   ___ Seldom   ___ Never

3. Makes decisions and executes policies:

___ Exceptionally well   ___ Very well   ___ Satisfactorily   ___ Never

4. According to subordinates, recognized and tries to reward meritorious achievement:

___ Nearly always   ___ Usually   ___ Sometimes   ___ Seldom   ___ Never

5. As confirmed by subordinates, possesses insight into their problems:

___ Nearly always   ___ Usually   ___ Sometimes   ___ Seldom   ___ Never

6. As evidenced by subordinates' attendance at workshops and conferences, actively encourages them to advance professionally:

___ Nearly always   ___ Usually   ___ Sometimes   ___ Seldom   ___ Never

7. From subordinates' point of view, delegates authority when appropriate:

___ Nearly always   ___ Usually   ___ Sometimes   ___ Seldom   ___ Never

COMMENTS AND OPPORTUNITY FOR RESPONSE

1. You are encouraged to comment on any elements of the position not specifically included in this form.

2. The faculty member under evaluation is invited to respond in writing.

Evaluator _____

Faculty member _____

Date _____

Wheaton College

**LIBRARY FACULTY
PERFORMANCE EVALUATION FORM**

NAME _____   RANK _____

DEPARTMENT _____   DATE _____

Job Description: _____ attached

This evaluation instrument will become part of the above identified Library Faculty member's dossier. Space is provided below for a narrative description of performance in broad categories.

1. Job performance (Consider the following: ability to think, ability to communicate, resourcefulness, emotional maturity, personality, administrative and supervisory responsibility where appropriate, etc.)

2. Professional development (Consider the following: research, publication, service in professional organizations, work toward additional graduate degrees, etc.)

Evaluator's signature _____   Title _____

Faculty member's signature _____

(Faculty member may respond in writing on reverse side of this form.)

9

APPENDIX C
PERFORMANCE EVALUATION REVIEW
DICK SMITH LIBRARY
TARLETON STATE UNIVERSITY

DATE: _____

NAME: _____   DEPARTMENT: _____
       (Last, First, Middle Initial)

TITLE: _____   PERIOD COVERED: _____

Check the appropriate blanks:

_____ Annual evaluation   _____ Self-evaluation

_____ Conditional/Probationary evaluation _____ Peer-evaluation

_____ Exit evaluation   _____ Supervisor

Purpose: To serve as a guide to individual growth and improvement as a professional librarian; to encourage critical self-evaluation and to facilitate constructive communication within the organization; to motivate the striving the excellence in service; to provide a performance history.

---

or final file copy:

Evaluee's signature _____ Date: _____

Supervisor's signature _____ Date: _____

A. GENERAL PERFORMANCE ASSESSMENT

	OUTSTANDING	EXCELLENT	SATISFACTORY	FAIR	UNSATISFACTORY	NOT APPLICABLE
1. Establishment of objectives and goals						
2. Formation of plans						
3. Execution of plans						
4. Knowledge beyond area of specialty						
5. Knowledge in area of specialty						
6. Familiar with the job description and its requirements						
7. Knowledge of current developments in field						
8. Overall knowledge and synthesis of library services						
9. Translation of University's academic programs into effective service						
10. Ability to make sound, objective decisions						
11. Innovation in methods and procedures						
12. Acts independently when appropriate						
13. Accuracy in the completion of tasks						
14. Accepts responsibility						
15. Is productive						
16. Strives for superior, quality performance						
17. Willingness to work beyond ordinary requirements						
18. Receptiveness to change, ideas of others, alternative approaches, criticism, etc.						
19. Prompt follow through on assignments						
20. Sets priorities and accomplishes important work first						
21. Is innovative and creative						
22. Demonstrates initiative						
23. Identifies problems and promotes their solutions						
24. Effectiveness in communicating with and dealing with:						
supervisor and other University administrators						
library staff, including student assistants						
faculty and staff						
University students						
community-at-large						
29. Quality of reference service						
30. Listening ability						
31. Oral presentation						
32. Quality of written reports and correspondence						
33. Participation in:						
library discussions and meetings						
faculty meetings and committee work						
other University activities						
36. Related study, research, writing, or other personal development activities						
37. Membership and participation in professional organizations						

B. SUPERVISORY PERFORMANCE

	O U T S T A N D I N G	E X C E L L E N T	S A T I S F A C T O R Y	F A I R	U N S A T I S F A C T O R Y	N O T A P P L I C A B L E
1. Welds staff into a unit with clearly recognized goals and objectives						
2. Is available to counsel and assist subordinates						
3. Recognizes and tries to reward meritorious achievement of subordinates						
4. Possesses insight into the problems encountered by subordinates in their work						
5. Is honest, dependable, and fair in dealings with subordinates						
6. Gives full credit for the ideas and work of subordinates						
7. Actively enourages subordinates to advance professionally						
8. Organizes and evaluates the execution of department objectives and goals						
9. Makes decisions and executes policies						
10. Delegates authority when appropriate						

C. Briefly explain in more detail any items from A or B, including the item number for each (additional pages may be used if needed).

D. Performance areas of this job not previously addressed.

E. Performance in meeting goals (attach "Action Plan" for each current goal)

F. Significant accomplishments or original contributions not a part of goals set for the year.

G. Supervisor's summary comments and recommendations.

H. Employee's response (not required).

APPENDIX D
GOALS ACTION PLAN

Please complete one (1) form for each goal

Date: _____

Name and Title: _____

Goal Statement:

Priority number ____ of ____ goals

Related Library Goals:

Related Job Responsibility:

Action steps (include names of other individuals involved and time frame):

Outcome measure/judgment (in the absence of quantifiable measures, state what qualitative judgments will be used to indicate achievement of the goal):

Budget implications:

Interim Review with Supervisor:

Final Evaluation:

Weighting of Criteria

Widener University
Chester, Pennsylvannia

State University of New York College at Geneseo
Geneseo, New York

GUIDELINES AND PROCEDURES FOR APPOINTMENTS, RETENTION, REDUCTION IN FORCE, PROMOTIONS, EXTENDED TERM APPOINTMENTS AND RENEWAL OF EXTENDED TERM APPOINTMENT OF LIBRARY FACULTY

WOLFGRAM MEMORIAL LIBRARY
WIDENER UNIVERSITY

A. Ranks of academic librarians and the criteria for eligibility:

1. Affiliate Librarian -- the entry level, minimum qualifications for which are the successful completion of a Masters Degree in Library or Information Science from an ALA accredited institution, or, in exceptional circumstances, another appropriate degree.

2. Assistant Librarian/Assistant Professor -- designating professional competence beyond the entry level. Qualifications should include: a minimum of three years professional experience and additional graduate courses relevant to subject specialization or other expertise, or continuing education through advanced workshops, internships, etc. It represents satisfactory performance in this or another academic library.

3. Associate Librarian/Associate Professor -- representing superior professional performance. Qualifications include a second graduate degree, or advanced degree beyond the Master in Library or Information Science, and six years of above average professional performance. (Only under appropriate circumstances can other criteria of publishing, research, etc., replace the educational requirements.)

4. Librarian/Professor -- the highest rank achieved only through superior performance as a professional librarian as well as through the completion of an appropriate degree beyond the Masters in Library or Information Science. It is to be given as an acknowledgement of exceptional contribution to the University of the profession. It cannot be given in less than five years in the Associate Librarian rank.

1

B. Appointment may be made at any librarian rank if the candidate meets the specific criteria. The job assignment of the individual does not depend on rank.

   1. Other forms of Appointment:

     Adjunct Librarian -- part-time and/or temporary assignment with professional duties. Normally they have the same educational requirements as Affiliate Librarian.

   2. Terms of Appointment:

     Appointments are made for the fiscal year. Guidelines for Library Faculty benefits shall follow University policies for traditional faculty.

C. Retention of Librarian prior to the Eligibility for Extended Term Appointment

   1. Criteria for retention should be based upon three fundamental principles:

     a) performance

     b) professional development, research and/or creativity

     c) service to the University, the profession and/or the community

7/92 2. To support retention, the following is required:

7/92   a. Self-evaluation

7/92   b. Performance review by the department head

7/92 3. Evaluation and performance review are forwarded to the Director.

7/92 4. The Director's recommendation shall be forwarded to the Provost.

D. Promotion, Extended Term Appointment, and Renewal of Extended Term Appointment

7/92 (see Appendix A)

7/92 1. Criteria for promotion, extended term appointment, and renewal of extended term appointment should be based upon the following fundamental principles:

     a. Professional Effectiveness

        i) Mastery of professional skills and techniques in one's assigned area (e.g. database searching, knowledge of vendors and jobbers, knowledge of

2

124 - Weighting of Criteria

AACRII and MARC formats, knowledge of general reference tools and those in one's area, exhibits)

ii) Provide teaching and learning resources in support of formal instruction (e.g. providing bibliographic instruction both formal and informal, acquisition and organization of materials, preparation of bibliographies, user guides or catalogs)

iii) Application of investigative studies advancing new methods, procedures, trends and technologies. For example, an awareness of computer applications, bibliographic control, management techniques

iv) Effective communications (oral and written with students, staff members and faculty)

v) Organization and administrative abilities (e.g. supervisory skills, time management)

vi) Participation in governance activities (University and/or Library committees)

b. Professional Development and Scholarly Achievement

i) Post master study in library science or additional formal or continuing education

ii) Attendance at conferences, workshops

iii) Membership in professional organizations

iv) Service to professional organizations in committee work (e.g. ALA, ACRL, PLA, TCLC, CHI)

v) Participation in conferences, seminars or workshops

vi) Publication or research

vii) Receipt of fellowships, grants, awards or other special honors

c) Contribution to the University or Community

i) Participation in community service activities

3

      ii)   Professional consultation

      iii) Participation in University affairs

Weight of categories:

    Professional Effectiveness 65%

    Professional Development and Scholarly Achievement 25%

    Contribution to the University/Community   10%

Percentage of total required for promotion

    Affiliate Librarian to Assistant 60%

    Assistant to Associate   75-80%

    Associate to Librarian   90%

Percentage of total required for extended term appointment 65-70%

2.   Promotion reviews and considerations for extended term appointment and renewal of extended term appointment should be conducted according to the Library Bylaws by a committee composed of peers.

3.   To support requirements for promotion and extended term appointment, the

7/92 following documentation is required:

    a.   Updated professional vitae

    b.   Candidate statement

7/92 c. Letter of recommendation from appropriate department head

7/92 d. Letter(s) of support from colleagues within the library and/or University colleagues

7/92 e. For promotion from Assistant to Associate: evidence of second graduate or advanced degree (e.g. certificate of advanced study in Information Studies)

7/92 Candidates may submit the following evidence:

    f.   Records of professional development and other related activities

    g.   Transcripts of courses taken and degree pursued

7/92 4. To support requirements for Renewal of Extended Term Appointment the following documentation is required:

4

126 - Weighting of Criteria

NUMERICAL RATING OF LIBRARIANS

Name of Person Under Evaluation_____

Name of Person Submitting Evaluation_____

A. PROFESSIONAL PERFORMANCE (WEIGHTING MUST = .8)

1. **Effectiveness in Performance** (Weighting = .5)
   Assess the candidate's performance of basic job
   responsibilities. Factors to be evaluated may
   include success, efficiency, and productivity in
   carrying out assigned duties; command of subject
   matter in assigned function; and willingness to
   accept increased responsibility and handle it
   successfully.

   Minimal
   1   2
   Fair
   · 3   4
   Good
   5   6
   Superior
   7   8
   Outstanding
   9   10
   ___ x .5 = ___

2. **Professional Ability** (Weighting = .2)
   Assess the candidate's professional qualities which
   facilitate effective performance. Factors to be
   evaluated may include organizational skills,
   communication skills, commitment to service,
   dependability, judgment, dedication, enthusiasm,
   initiative, creativity, and ability to work
   effectively with colleagues. Professional ability
   may be demonstrated by reorganization of departments
   or functions to increase efficiency, introduction
   of innovative services or procedures, or preparation
   of library publications, training materials, or
   internal reports.

   Minimal
   1   2
   Fair
   3   4
   Good
   5   6
   Superior
   7   8
   Outstanding
   9   10
   ___ x .2 = ___

3. <u>Continuing Professional Growth</u> (Weighting = .1)
Assess the candidate's degree of commitment to ongoing
professional development. Factors to be evaluated may
include continuing education, attendance at workshops
and conferences, additional postgraduate degrees, and
membership and participation in professional organizations.

Minimal
1   2
Fair
3   4
Good
5   6
Superior
7   8
Outstanding
9   10
____ x .1 =____

B. CONTRIBUTIONS TO THE PROFESSION   (Weighting = .1)
Assess the candidate's formal contributions to librarianship
relative to rank and stage of career. Factors to be evaluated
may include lectures or papers presented at professional
workshops or conferences, offices held or other active participation in professional organizations, consulting work, grant
seeking, research (including research in progress), scholarly
publications, honors, awards, or reputation among colleagues
and in the profession.

Minimal
1   2
Fair
3   4
Good
5   6
Superior
7   8
Outstanding
9   10
____ x .1 =____

C. EFFECTIVENESS IN UNIVERSITY AND COMMUNITY SERVICE (Weighting = .1)
Assess the candidate's degree of commitment to service, within
and beyond the college community. Factors to be evaluated may
include successful committee work, participation in campus and
University governance, and involvement in campus or University
related student or community activities.

Minimal
1   2
Fair
3   4
Good
5   6
Superior
7   8
Outstanding
9   10
____ x .1 =__

FORM H1-L

Supplement to Faculty Handbook

Winthrop University
Rock Hill, South Carolina

CRITERIA FOR TENURE
AS APPLIED TO WINTHROP UNIVERSITY LIBRARY FACULTY
Adopted October 15, 1979
Revised August 20, 1984
Revised August 13, 1992
Revised January 22, 1993

Introduction

Winthrop University Library faculty who are candidates for tenure must meet the general qualifications for tenure as outlined in the Winthrop University Manual for Faculty Members which is in effect at the time of candidacy. The purpose of these criteria is to define the terms "teaching effectiveness" and "scholarly attainment and professional recognition" as they apply to librarians.

Fundamental Considerations

The librarian's academic preparation for an appointment to the library faculty is established on the basis of the terminal professional degree from an American Library Association accredited library school.

In order to be considered for tenure, an individual must consistently perform at a high level in areas which contribute to the educational mission of the university, as well as in those areas which contribute to the effective administration of the library organization. Evidence of level of performance may be adduced from the judgments of colleagues on the library faculty, from members of the larger academic community, and/or from professional colleagues outside the academic institution.

Formal classroom instruction is only one of many types of teaching activity in which academic librarians are engaged. The bulk of a librarian's time is usually spent on activities which directly support the entire teaching mission of the university. The candidate's abilities in developing the library collection, and interpreting the collection to library users in informal, one-to-one interactions will be given primary emphasis during the evaluation process.

Traditional publications as well as workshops, symposia, institutes, seminars, meetings of regional and national organizations, etc., are the primary means of communications within the discipline. Therefore, a candidate's contributions in any of these areas will be recognized.

Finally, particular consideration will be given to the candidate's potential for continuing growth and contributions to the university.

Specific Criteria

Any candidate for tenure should present evidence of his or her effectiveness in the following two areas (the examples listed below are in no particular order):

1. <u>Contributions to the education function of the university (teaching):</u>
for example,
teaching, including, but not limited to individualized instruction, classroom instruction, library orientation, or preparation of instructional media;
activities as defined by the responsibilities listed in the individual's position description; speeches or special presentations to university classes and groups.

2. <u>Activities related to scholarly attainment and professional recognition:</u>
for example,
books, bibliographies or articles in proceedings or scholarly journals;
publication of special catalogs, indexes, or guides to library resources;
editorship or membership on editorial boards of journals, newsletters, and the like;
officer of a national, regional or state professional organization, chair of a committee of a national professional organization;
presentation of papers, or performance at workshops, institutes, or seminars; reviews, abstracts, or translations of books or other literature;
formal consulting;
service as a member of a team of experts, task force, review committee, or similar body;
member of a committee of a national professional association, chair of a committee of a regional or state professional organization;
pursuit of additional degrees, or participation in continuing education or other academic programs designed to enhance one's area of specialization;
member of a committee of a regional or state professional organization;

creative works including, but not limited to exhibitions and audiovisual presentations.

recipient of grants/fellowships or professional awards

A candidate should also document service to the university as further evidence of his or her suitability for tenure:

3. <u>Service to the university (academic responsibility)</u>: for example, service as member or chairman of library faculty and university committees;

sponsorship or advisement of student groups;

participation in honorary or academic societies;

service to the community which utilizes the expertise of the faculty member;

speeches and special presentations to community groups.

CRITERIA FOR PROMOTION
AS APPLIED TO WINTHROP UNIVERSITY LIBRARY FACULTY
Adopted October 15, 1979
Revised August 20, 1984
Revised August 13, 1992
Revised January 22, 1993

Introduction

Winthrop University Library faculty who are candidates for promotion must meet the general qualifications for promotion as outlined in the Winthrop University Manual for Faculty Members which is in effect at the time of candidacy. The purpose of these criteria is to define the terms teaching, scholarship, professional service and academic responsibility as they apply to librarians.

Fundamental Considerations

The librarian's academic preparation for an appointment to the library faculty is established on the basis of the terminal professional degree.

In order to be considered for promotion, an individual must consistently perform at a high level in areas which contribute to the educational mission of the university, as well as in those areas which contribute to the effective administration of the library organization. Evidence of level of performance may be adduced from the judgments of colleagues on the library faculty, from members of the larger academic community, and/or from professional colleagues outside the academic institution.

Formal classroom instruction is only one of many types of teaching activity in which academic librarians are engaged. The bulk of a librarian's time is usually spent on activities which directly support the entire teaching mission of the university. The candidate's abilities in developing the library collection, and interpreting the collection to library users in informal, one-to-one interactions will be given primary emphasis during the evaluation process.

Traditional publications as well as workshops, symposia, institutes, seminars, meetings of regional and national organizations, et., are the primary means of communications within the discipline. Therefore, a candidate's contributions in any of these areas will be recognized.

It should be noted that academic rank is not dependent upon the faculty member's position within the organization.

Specific Criteria

All candidates for promotion in rank will present evidence of their activities in the following areas. Candidates for the senior ranks (Associate Professor and Professor) are expected to display increasing levels of activity in all areas, with emphasis on quality of contribution.

The examples listed under each item below are in no particular order.

1. <u>Contributions to the education function of the university (teaching)</u>: for example,
teaching, including, but not limited to individualized instruction, classroom instruction, library orientation, or preparation of instructional media;
activities as defined by the responsibilities listed in the individual's position description;
speeches or special presentations to university classes and groups.

2. <u>Activities related to inquiry and research (scholarship)</u>: for example,
publications such as books, bibliographies, or articles in professional or scholarly journals;
publication of special catalogs, indexes, or guides to library resources;
editorship or membership on editorial boards of journals, newsletters, and the like;
presentation of papers, or performance at workshops, institutes, or seminars;
reviews, abstracts, or translations of books or other literature;
formal consulting;
service as a member of a team of experts, task force, review committee, or similar body;
pursuit of additional degrees, or participation in continuing education or other programs designed to enhance one's area of specialization;
creative works including, but not limited to exhibitions and audiovisual presentations.
recipient of grants/fellowships or professional awards

3. <u>Contributions to the advancement of the profession (professional service):</u>

for example,

active participation in professional or learned societies as a member, officer, committee member, or committee chairman;

organization of workshops, institutes, seminars;

other substantive contributions to the profession at large.

4. <u>Service to the university (academic responsibility):</u>

for example,

service as member or chairman of library faculty and university committees;

sponsorship or advisement of student groups;

participation in honorary or academic societies;

service to the community which utilizes the expertise of the faculty member;

speeches and special presentation to community groups.

External Evaluation

State University of New York College at New Paltz
New Platz, New York

Appendix A

SUNY COLLEGE AT NEW PALTZ
Library Faculty

EXTERNAL EVALUATION FOR
PROMOTION AND CONTINUING APPOINTMENT
GUIDELINES

I. **PERSONNEL ACTIONS FOR WHICH EXTERNAL EVALUATIONS ARE REQUIRED:**
Decisions on continuing appointment and on promotion to Full Librarian
and on promotion to Associate Librarian.

II. **IDENTIFICATION OF EXTERNAL EVALUATORS:**
External evaluators must be established librarian scholars or practitioners in the field or fields of the faculty candidate's specialization. Ordinarily, external evaluators should be senior tenured
librarians at recognized universities and colleges or senior staff at research institutes. It may be more appropriate to seek out similarly
qualified professional persons or practitioners connected with other
types of institutions and with different, but substantial qualifications
in their fields. However, at least one reviewer must be connected with
an institution of higher education and be familiar with commonly accepted
standards for tenure and promotion. External reviewers must not be
former teachers, colleagues, research associates or personal friends, nor
should they be people who have evaluated the candidate in the past,
either at New Paltz or at another institution. Acceptable external
evaluators may have a previous professional acquaintance with the faculty
candidate's work.

III. **SELECTION OF EXTERNAL EVALUATORS:**
The most common manner of selecting external evaluators is for the
library faculty candidate and his/her Director to work closely together
on the matter. The candidate should suggest the names of potential
evaluators who meet the criteria stated in II above; five potential
evaluators is a useful number to start with. The Director may add to the
names received from the candidate and then select the two names that the
Director and candidate believe will best serve the purpose of evaluating
the candidate's work. The Director should contact prospective evaluators
as soon as possible to ascertain their willingness to serve in this
capacity.

Should the candidate choose not to participate in the process of selecting external evaluators, it shall be the responsibility of the Director
to do so. The Director may consult with the candidate and/or the department chair concerning the selection of external evaluators. It is the
responsibility of the candidate to inform the Director in a timely manner
that he/she wishes the Director to perform this function.

The Administration may on its own initiative seek supplementary external
evaluation if it is deemed that a particular personnel decision requires
such action.

IV. **MATERIALS FOR REVIEW BY EXTERNAL EVALUATORS:**
External evaluators are most helpful in assessing the work of a faculty candidate when the evaluator's attention is directed toward materials that can be evaluated by someone who will be unfamiliar with the College at New Paltz. It may be important for evaluators to assess the candidate's service to the discipline and/or to well-defined constituencies external to the College at New Paltz if such service can be sufficiently documented.

The candidate's resume should always be included. It might be useful for the candidate to write a brief narrative describing his/her achievements in the several categories considered at the College in evaluating faculty for major personnel actions. Such narratives assist evaluators in understanding the College and the constraints under which the candidate may have to function. The narratives further aid external evaluators in comparing the College to others with the evaluator may be familiar.

V. **FORMAL REQUEST TO EXTERNAL EVALUATOR:**
When materials for evaluation such as those described in IV above have been gathered, they should be sent to the external evaluators under cover of a letter that requests the evaluator to address specific questions concerning the material. A pertinent question could be:

Does the candidate's work show development beyond that normally expected or required in the rank presently occupied?

A sample cover letter is attached.

VI. **CONFIDENTIALITY:**
External evaluators must be given the opportunity to submit their evaluations in complete confidence. The cover letter to an external evaluator must contain the following:

In your response, will you please address the issue of the confidentiality of your evaluation in the following manner:

1) May the candidate read this recommendation?   yes/no

2) May the candidate read this recommendation if
   all identification as to its source is deleted?   yes/no

If the respondent does not reply to the above questions, or if the respondent's reply is negative, the statement of the external reviewer shall not be made available to the candidate.

All external evaluations are to be considered by Library sub-committees and the Library Director in the process of making recommendations for major personnel actions. Care must be taken during such review to preserve the confidentiality of those external evaluators who may have requested it.

External evaluations are to be included in all copies of the candidate's
file to be considered in the personnel action. If an evaluator has
requested strict confidentiality, the evaluation should be placed in an
envelope marked "confidential" and added to the file. Letters from
evaluators requesting only that identifying elements be removed should be
so treated and included in the file.

On the matter of such confidential communications, see the UUP Agreement,
Article 31.2 (b).

VII. TIME-TABLE FOR SOLICITING EXTERNAL EVALUATIONS:

Be aware that soliciting external evaluations takes time: time to contact potential evaluators, time to gather and send materials, time to
receive a response. The process should be started as early as possible.
External evaluators should be informed of the time-frame for a response.
An evaluator should be given a specific deadline for a response in the
cover letter. The files of candidates being considered for personnel actions in the spring (when most cases requiring external evaluations are
reviewed) are due to the Central Committee early in March. Therefore,
external reviewers should be identified and in possession of materials to
review before the end of the Fall Term.

Should you have questions about the process of soliciting external
evaluations, please confer with the Vice President for Academic Affairs.

3/31/89